Dark Side
of the
Mood

Dark Side
of the
Mood

A Journey Through
Bipolar Disorder to Recovery

Sheri Medford

Bahá'í
PUBLISHING

Wilmette, Illinois

Bahá'í Publishing
401 Greenleaf Avenue, Wilmette, Illinois 60091

17   16   15   14   4   3   2   1

Library of Congress Cataloging-in-Publication Data

Medford, Sheri.
  Dark side of the mood : a journey through bipolar disorder to recovery / Sheri
Medford.
     pages cm
  Includes bibliographical references.
  ISBN 978-1-61851-071-6 (alk. paper)
  1. Medford, Sheri—Mental health. 2. Manic-depressive persons—United
States—Biography. I. Title.
  RC516.M423 2014
  616.89'50092—dc23
  [B]
                                        2014024012

Book design by Patrick Falso
Cover design by Misha Maynerick Blaise
Cover photograph by Ron Crowl

*Dedicated to my parents, my brother Jim,
and my husband Bill.*

Contents

Journal Entry: The Dream 3

Introduction 7

Denial 11

Acknowledgment 41

Acceptance 99

Recovery 155

Appendix A 183

Appendix B 193

Appendix C 197

Journal Entry: The Dream

Age thirteen. My dream, enveloped in an empty silence, had no color—only the black, grays, and white of an old snapshot. My parents, my brother, and I walked down a straight paved street. We walked, not looking at each other, not looking from side to side—seeing nothing, aware of nothing but the asphalt road. No choices. Time oozed by.

Without comment, my brother and I, like two souls in one body, turned away from our parents onto a dirt road. A gold tone highlighted the muted landscape forming in the distance.

With no warning, leaving the shared path, intent unknown, I hiked alone into a succulent and voracious jungle. A dense darkness drew me in. Branches slapped me, thorns scratched me, shadows hid the ground under my feet. I stumbled. I grabbed and clutched at shadows thinking they had substance. The journey felt endless in its devouring silence. Desperately I clawed at the darkness.

Then I found an opening leading out of the jungle.

I emerged into soft, warm sunlight where a large valley held a still lake in its palm. I passed by an oddly familiar cabin to the lake's edge. I sat, took off my shoes and socks, rolled up my jeans, and eagerly submerged my feet in the silken water. I peered into the clear water where glistening multicolored rocks lay nestled together. I felt an incredible glory as I looked up and saw the iridescent mountain reflecting an ancient mystic silence.

Introduction

Bipolar disorder takes me to a place I call *the Nothingness*. It is more than depression, more than mania. It lurks inside of me like a parasite. The doctors say it will never go away and I am now ready to accept that truth. It is a process that has no finish line, except physical death. If I win the battle, I will someday die of natural causes and not from the Nothingness.

In 1985, my parents picked me up in Spokane, Washington, after I was hospitalized for a suicide attempt. When we reached Roseburg, Oregon, we drove five miles out into the country where dad had built their dream house. Everything looked familiar until I read the street sign. "Mom look, the street's name has been changed!" Strange, my doctor had just diagnosed me with "bipolar disorder" (manic depression), and now someone had changed my parents' home street to Hi Lo Lane. The irony didn't escape me—Hi Lo Lane. Oh well, stranger things have happened, and that is what this story is about.

Dark Side of the Mood technically started in 1975 during my first hospitalization, but at that point I had been filling a drawer with notes and quotes about my problems for years. I drew a lot of this book from that drawer. I have actually had five hospitalizations to date. The years in between these hospitalizations were filled with periods of three to four months of depression, followed by shorter periods of mania. I didn't put everything down on paper because it was cycle after cycle, more of the same.

Over the years, medications changed, counselors changed, locations changed, but the illness was always there—relentless.

An invisible disability like bipolar disorder disrupts the rhythm of a life. Without a socially acceptable rhythm it is difficult, if not impossible, to find a comfortable place in the world.

Everything in life has a rhythm. Our rhythm must resonate with society, otherwise a disconnect can occur, creating a dysfunctional life. In the individual life, a person's rhythm is not the only problem; society itself creates obstacles. We must understand both personal and social rhythms, and how they interact. What follows is my story of a life disrupted.

Denial

EUGENE, OREGON
1975
AGE 25

"Only to the extent that we expose ourselves over and over to annihilation can that which is indestructible be found in us."
—Buddhist Teaching

Chapter 1

"Does it not appear as if one who lived habitually on one side of the pain threshold might need a different sort of religion from one who habitually lives on the other?"
—William James

So, I'm resourceful! Some counselor! Why can't he realize resourcefulness has nothing to do with this? This is the beginning of the Nothingness, and when I'm there, I have no control. He can't see the change coming. He can't feel it growing. Resourcefulness, what a laugh! How can a human quality help when I turn into a shadow?

I drifted through the emptiness of the hospital corridor, mesmerized by the light streaming through the distant glass entranceway. As I moved closer, I saw dust particles dancing intimately with the sunlight. I stood motionless, envying the dust, knowing I could not dance, recognizing my desire to avoid the light—for what would happen to a shadow if surrounded by light?

A strong impulse to hide pushed me through the women's room door. I pressed my back against the cool gray tile and as I slid into the corner, my panic left with a sigh. Listening to the quiet, I became a small girl again, believing life was controllable. Safe.

The hinged door swung open. Click, click, click of heels on tile—an intruder.

I won't look. I won't give in. More noises, rustles of fabric, click, click to the sink. When will those feet leave? Click, click; they hurried by and were gone. Safe again.

What crazy thinking—did I think the Nothingness wouldn't follow me here? It was there with me and outside the door waiting. The Nothingness reached beyond time-space. There was no safe place. There never had been. There never would be.

I glanced up, looking for a clue to survival. On the bottom of the washroom sink stamped in blue on white porcelain, I read the words "American Standard." What's the American Standard for a sink or a human being? I didn't know the standard anymore. Once, I thought I did.

When I was younger, the standard of pretty and smart appeared as solid as a floor. I wasn't worried about smart, I knew I was OK there but I wondered about pretty. I often analyzed my face in the mirror of my childhood bathroom. I liked my hair—auburn was magic, brown until the sun turned it red and gold. My face from the front gave me little grief, as long as I didn't smile big, which made my nose pop out like a zoom lens on a camera. Oh, but my profile! Mom used to call me her Queen Nephritides. This seemed a great thing to her but I knew about that Egyptian queen, dead and buried for centuries in a pyramid. A mummy's profile, now that concerned me.

The prettiness standard didn't pay off. That floor I stood upon had trapdoors everywhere, dumping me over and over into the Nothingness. I always ended up empty and hiding. No standard I tried would hold my weight.

A touch on my shoulder brought me back to my present hiding place. I looked up at a nurse who had a ceremonial mask of empathy plastered on her face. She obviously thought she knew what I needed when she killed the silence, "Sheri, you need to go home and have some lunch."

How could she know what I needed? She had only her perception of me and I knew how false perceptions could be.

She pulled me to my feet and led me to the hospital entrance. I held my breath and tried to ignore the dancing dust. Her white uniform and the way she moved told me she felt important. She had found a place in the world. How could she live in this world of jagged edges? The same world shredded me. "What is so different about me?" I thought. I had no answer and no choice but to walk through the door into the light.

Weirdness surrounded me as I drove home in my VW Bug. The town and its commotion had no meaning. Only the void that held the planet as its prisoner felt familiar. I checked my rearview mirror for traffic, and noticed my brow sewn together with tension. My arms and legs drove in automatic, my mind suspended, clinging to past memories.

I had some wonderful memories of my childhood, but even then I knew the sense of control everyone walked around with was a distortion. People worked and shopped as though they had no other purpose. Reality invisible, they lived for the shopping mall— a black hole that sucked them into psychic oblivion.

I believed in a reality beyond credit cards, beyond appearances. Though I experienced it only briefly many years ago, its memory lovingly haunted me.

I was a fifth grader in my school cafeteria competing in a chicken-eating contest. Absorbed in the thought of winning, I raked large hunks of chicken, skin and all, into my mouth, tossed the bones with one hand while stuffing more meat to my mouth with the other. I ate intensely. Then abruptly, simultaneously, time stretched like a rubber band pulled to its full extension by giant hands. I existed in two places at once: in the cafeteria, and in those giant hands outside of time. In that extended moment my awareness grew into immensity. I felt huge in comparison to my normal tiny self. My eyes saw, though I don't know how, the lunchroom, the neighborhood, the state, the country, the world, and beyond. A wordless voice communicated, "NO MATTER WHAT THEY TELL YOU ABOUT GOD, IT'S TOO LIMITED." Then the giant hands let go of the rubber band and I snapped back into the small me.

I felt a jab in my ribs and heard a laugh from the boy next to me. "You win!"

The other children ran at the sound of the school bell, but I sat with eyes fixed on the pile of chicken bones while thinking about the message. I never questioned the source of the voice. I knew it spoke the truth—a gift that might one day save me.

After that, whenever my senses closed in on me, I would reach out for those giant hands to feel the Fullness. Not a fullness of eating chicken, but of seeing the wholeness of things where everyone and everything was safe.

My thoughts returned from the past as I pulled into my driveway. I sat in my VW Bug, like a canned vegetable, thinking how unreal the sky appeared, as if I could scratch the clouds off with a fingernail and peel back the blue like cellophane. I prayed for those wonderful hands, but nothing happened. I was alone.

I entered my apartment, darkened behind pulled shades, a place where no plant could grow. I had learned the hard way that any plant I cared for would die. Mother had given me an African violet for my birthday a few months back but not wanting to watch it die, I put it in the closet.

I looked around at the living room full of furniture, nothing matching, nothing elegant: tattered couch, a paint-peeled green chair, bricks and boards with deranged stacks of books. Everything was too small for the room and failed to hang together in a cozy way—only shapes to fill empty space. No carpet, no pictures on the walls, I should have hated it but I didn't care. Comfort wasn't an issue. The Nothingness didn't give a rip about my comfort.

I went to the kitchen, searching wearily in the stacks of dirty dishes for the cleanest looking glass. Wanting only to sleep, I took two of the pills prescribed by my doctor.

As I walked into the bedroom to hide inside sleep, the mirror nailed on the wall fell and shattered at my feet. With great tenacity my mind tried to make sense of the event. "See the shattered pieces of your life." Fearful my world had no meaning, I stepped over the shards and flopped onto my bed. Rapidly a warm drowsiness rolled over me. "These are good pills!"

"Shit! " I screamed as the radio blared the time of day. My fingers counted wildly. Oh God, I missed work!

I grabbed the phone, "Please, it's important that I talk to Dr. Campbell!" I rocked back and forth, cradling my stomach, as I always did when freefalling into the Nothingness.

"Sheri, what's the problem?" The doctor sounded rushed but concerned.

Words spilled out. "It's the day before Thanksgiving, those pills knocked me out, I missed work, I don't have a turkey, and the mirror broke—everything's a mess! My parents are coming, they'll see my mess!"

The doctor's slow, controlled tone interrupted, "Sheri, calm down. Take some slow deep breaths. Don't worry, you don't have to deal with anything right now. Pack some clothes and get someone to take you to the hospital emergency room. Can you do that? I'll call and let them know you're coming. You'll be fine."

The doctor's voice reassured me. I stopped rocking. "Thank you, doctor, thank you! The people at the hospital can help me, can't they?"

"I'll drop in later and see how you're doing. You'll be fine." I heard the click and hung up.

Scurrying, I shoved clothes from the floor into a black plastic trash bag. Life was a crazy maze, I thought, but I could learn to find my way.

With no friends to call, I drove myself the five blocks to the hospital. I kept saying aloud, "You're fine. You're fine." I tried to overpower the inner whisper shouting at me, "You will never make it out of the Nothingness alive!"

Chapter 2

I didn't know who she was. She didn't give her name and she wasn't
interested in mine or in anything about me. Not even a nurse, just
someone the hospital paid to go through my things. I felt like a
criminal.

"Why do you have two razors in your bag?"

For some reason I felt guilty. "I guess it was a mistake."

"I'll need a promise from you, young lady, that you will check
out of the hospital first, should you decide to commit suicide."

I stared, mouth open.

"Well?"

"Ah, yes, I promise." So, I realized, the hospital had no escape
plan against the Nothingness either—only more punishment. Bars
clanged shut in my mind.

She pushed my bag at me from her side of the counter. After
tagging my hairdryer and the two razors with name and patient
number, she locked them up. As I took my bag and tried to smile,
it astonished me to hear myself thank her. Submissively, I followed
her to an isolation room with nothing but a round table, a row
of stacked molded orange chairs, and a wall mirror along the op-
posing wall. I wondered if the eyes behind the mirror would diag-
nose me depressed or potentially violent just by watching me sit.
Would they think I looked crazy? Or, worse, maybe I was but they
wouldn't notice.

"You can join the other patients after three days of observation."
she said. "There's the bathroom and you'll sleep in that room." She

pointed to a small adjoining room, turned, and left, closing the door behind her.

Three days rolled into eternity while I tried not to look like a lunatic. I felt immense empathy for the animals at the zoo, with nothing to do but sit and be scrutinized by strangers. The first day, they did give me a psychological test called the MMPI, which took two hours. It asked questions like, "Do you prefer tall women?" I wondered if I should have a preference. Other than that, I sat.

The nights were horrid. The nurse came in each night and gave me a pill that glued my neurons together until I couldn't move; even to get out of bed to go to the bathroom. In my nightmares, killer shadows stalked me while my feet couldn't connect with the ground and my screams made no sound. I told the nurse about the amorphous creatures undulating grotesquely around my bed all night, and begged her not to give me the pill. She apologized warmly, telling me the trip to hell every night was hospital regulations.

My last day in isolation, the Gestapo woman from the ER led a string bean of a man into the room. I panicked, thinking, "How do they know he's not dangerous? What if he goes berserk while the doctors are out on a coffee break?"

"Hi, I'm Jerry." His smile lit up his tired and drawn face. A drug addict, he told me about his past experiences at this hospital and I swapped my novice story with him. A kind of connecting happened between us, and because I believed strongly in the mentor system of learning, Jerry became my nuthouse mentor.

Later that afternoon, a nurse said I could go to the main unit, but it seemed a dubious privilege. Jerry had two more days in isolation, and I would have to fend for myself in a strange new territory. As I walked down the hallway, I peeked into the rooms, which looked like dorm rooms at the University of Oregon, each with twin beds, matching spreads, and a small bathroom—pretty nice accommodations, considering.

A nurse introduced me to my roommate, a large woman with long, coarse, red hair that clashed against her red-plaid polyester suit. She didn't look crazy, but still I felt leery. "Just my luck to land a latent psychotic for a roommate," I thought. Her name was Carol and she offered me a tour of the unit.

The living room looked nothing like a hospital. The drapes and couches had fabric of fresh blues and sea greens—cool colors to promote calm behavior, I surmised. *Time* magazines, going back years, piled on the tables. Ashtrays everywhere, cigarette smoke burned my eyes. The patients looked like statues carved into the furniture. Their eyes were vacant. Were mine? The eerie quiet made my heart solidify.

The staff wore street clothes like undercover cops. Only the stethoscopes and blood pressure cuffs signaled that they were staff. The hospital had taken great pains to conceal the stark reality of what happens here. There was even a cute little kitchen with coffee and oatmeal cookies—everything for comfort, but I didn't feel at all comfortable.

After Carol left to see her doctor, I found an empty chair in the corner of the living room and waited.

Chapter 3

"You are obviously depressed." Dr. Randall flung her ponytail over the back of the chair as she sat down. She looked mature, despite hair past her waist. I could see the years of hard work in her eyes. We sat nearly knee to knee in the closet-sized room, studying each other. I felt a twinge of hope as she smiled warmly.

I imitated her smile.

She crossed her legs and sat forward. "I am starting you on two medications, Sheri. Stelazine is a tranquilizer and Sinequan is a mood elevator. Do you have any questions about either of these drugs?" She noticed my head shaking no and continued, "Now, Sheri, tell me about your depression."

My stomach knotted. I tried to think of some simple way to explain. "I've had other depressions. I don't know exactly when they started, but I think about 1972 after my divorce. I was twenty-one. I went off the 'pill' and it stopped my periods. After no period for over a year, my gynecologist put me on hormones to jumpstart my ovaries. I started my periods again, but I became addicted to Fig Newtons and gained 30 pounds." I shrugged away my blush.

I gulped air and continued. "In the past, the depression would lift after my period—snap, like a window shade going up—all of a sudden I would see everything clearer and brighter. It's like everything is out of focus, then boom, it's in focus. The difference always shocks me. I'd stop crying and stop eating handfuls of cookies. I then cleaned up my apartment and washed my hair. I'd be OK for two weeks. Not this time. "

"Go on."

I adjusted myself nervously. "I'm so tired." Tears spread over my cheeks. "My mind is numb, nothing feels real. Now, I don't know what I'll do if I can't count on the two weeks of feeling good. That's how I kept from flunking out of school. I'd work hard those two weeks to make up incompletes. I didn't usually need much sleep then. Now, I can't sleep enough and my job suffers because they demand consistency. Anne, one of the women I work with, gets mad at me a lot. She says I'm immature." I stopped for a moment, gathering the surfacing pain. "She's probably right, but I can't help it. I always really try. It completely controls me."

"What controls you?"

"I wish I knew. I try new angles to prevent the depressions—you know, vitamins, exercise, meditation. The results never change. I can't change it by trying. The Nothingness always wins."

"The Nothingness?" She looked up from her notes. "What's that?"

"It's something inside me, or beyond me, that steals my life. I only know what it does to my mind. It takes over and I have no say in the matter."

"You're not the only one who has recurrent depressions, Sheri. It's quite common in fact. I wish I had an answer for you now, but it may take some time." She got up and opened the door. "I will talk with you again tomorrow."

Chapter 4

The next morning I woke in a daze. Carol, dressed already, greeted me with a smile, her arm hanging awkwardly because of paralysis. She had arrived by ambulance a few weeks back, totally paralyzed. Her doctor called it hysteria and I wondered how she felt about that. If the Nothingness hadn't sat on my emotions, I would have felt closer to her. The Nothingness surely had her in its grip as well. I forced a smile as I rolled out of bed, heading for the bathroom, looking for solitude. The warm shower renewed my hope of feeling good again soon. The water flooded my face, distracting me from the dull ache inside. The night before, I had done my laundry for the first time in over a month. An accomplishment I felt proud of, because keeping clean took effort. I blotted dry with a towel, slipped into clean jeans and a sweatshirt, but skipped the makeup. My face still meant nothing to me.

Everyone stood around the med nurse in the main room getting their morning fix. I walked by.

"Sheri, I have some medications for you this morning." She smiled as she held out a Dixie cup.

"Here comes my membership in the walking dead club," I thought as I tossed the pills in my mouth. As I drank them down, I looked up at the nurse's face. Her expression was calm, but then, why not? She drugged people every day.

After breakfast, classes began and no one could avoid class. First there was relaxation—redundant since I'd just taken a huge dose of tranquilizers. Then assertiveness, crafts, and some kind of embarrassing field trip in a van with all the inmates—like bowling, ugh!

No one was allowed to be alone. Ever.

At 11:00 p.m., I took my Dixie cup of pills and got ready for bed. After lights out, I laid in bed on a cloud of drugs, drifting off to sleep. Suddenly a light hit my face and I sat up with a start.

"Don't worry, Sheri," a shadowy figure said from the doorway. "I'm the night nurse, it's my job to check on each patient every half hour. I flash the light on you to see if you're still breathing."

I collapsed back onto the bed in disbelief. "Great!"

Journal Entry

I dreamed of eating cookies and chocolate stolen from a safe at the edge of the ocean.

I hung on to a pole as I ate, to keep from being swept away by a huge wave. Mom ran along the rocky beach in a nurse's uniform, frantic to help.

Chapter 5

Journal Entry
Pain acts like acid that works on boundaries, barriers to consciousness, and if allowed, it will eat away the anger, eat away the ego.

Dr. Randall closed the door and sat across from me. As she leaned forward, I recalled from my Intervention Techniques 101 class in college that her forward body position showed empathy and interest.

"Sheri, I want to know more about your history. Tell me about your family."

I sat quietly for a moment. What would she think if I told her that whenever I closed my eyes, my mother's face looked back at me? It seemed I struggled continually to discover the *me* apart from *her*.

"Well, Mom's small physically but she has a strong personality. I don't think she realizes how big an impact she makes on my life. Everybody that I know of likes her. I don't think she knows that either." I thought for a moment. "I don't think she's ever recovered from her childhood really. Her mother died on an abortion table while she waited in the car. Mom was only four years old when she was left with her alcoholic father. She never talks about it, but I think she still feels abandoned. I feel her pain."

"How do you feel about her pain?"

I held my stomach and rocked back and forth. "I want to take it for her."

"What would she think of that?"

"I don't know. I'm sure she doesn't know how I feel. For a long time, I believed she didn't like me. I even asked her once, and she said if she had had a mother she'd have appreciated her more. I asked how I could know she had feelings if she never showed them. After all, I was her kid, right?" I shrugged. "One night we were in my room late, and she cried. She said she thought she had to be perfect. She frightened me. I could feel the room fill up with a terrified four-year-old girl."

"Does your mother have depressions?"

"The only one I know of for sure occurred after she gave birth to me. She said it lasted two years. Other than that, I don't know. She doesn't let on about her feelings."

"How would you like your relationship with your mother to change?"

I bit my lip. "Talk more, I guess, but like I said, she says it's too painful. I want to share her fears. I love her a lot." I smiled through my tears.

Six chronically depressed elderly women, a hostile pregnant teenager, a suicidal intellectual, Jerry the addict, and I, made up my first group therapy experience.

The depressed women all looked like muffins from the same muffin tin. They had washed-out facial features and were extremely polite and sweet natured. I wondered if that was their problem. The muffins' depressions had put them in the hospital many times.

The group exercise that day consisted of one partner talking for five minutes, then the other partner reflecting back the feelings expressed. My partner Barry, the intellectual, surprised me. His hair and skin were muted like a once-bright piece of cloth left out too long in the sun, which clashed with the dramatic multiple scars that ran horizontally across both wrists and up his arm. He talked about it freely.

"I don't know how many times I've attempted suicide or even why. I have a wonderful wife and two children I love very much. Things go really well for months but then I flip out and slit my wrists."

When I talked to people like Barry, my fairness theory of reality would run into a dead end. I shook my head to dissolve the image of an evil God imparting senseless brutal punishment. I wanted to believe in logical cause and effect—that those who suffered deserved it, but it just wasn't true. I couldn't be sure, but maybe Barry, smart as he was, saw too much of reality, where others only saw the surfaces of things.

Journal Entry

One of my problems is whenever I meet a new person I wonder what part of reality they've figured out that I haven't. When others might ask about business or politics, I ask what they think of the universe, life, consciousness. What's the purpose of it all? I suspect the source of this urge to understand is my feeling so alone. I'm preoccupied with the meaning of things. As a child I saw the wonder in rocks, animals, everything. That's normal for a child, but unlike others, as my life grew in complexity, I couldn't dull my senses and the wonder completely overtook me.

Chapter 6

Dr. Randall entered the room smiling. "You look as though you're feeling better today. The medication must be helping. Don't you think?"

I wondered how she could think the medication was helping, instead of the Nothingness taking a short vacation. We always see what we want.

"I guess so. I do feel better. I started my period last night; I usually feel better then."

"Today I want to hear about your father." She hesitated, then asked, "Why the nervous look? What's that all about?"

"Well, it's hard to know what to say."

"Tell me about your childhood memories of him."

"Most of my childhood didn't stick in my brain, it was so bland."

"Close your eyes and relax. Talk about anything that comes to mind."

I leaned back, my eyes closed, searching for a memory. I remembered Dad laughing, stamping his feet, shaking sawdust from his gray sweatshirt, his black wavy hair snowing fine yellow sawdust on Mom's clean linoleum floor.

I opened my eyes. "Mom always got mad at him when he wouldn't punish me. I'd do something cute and get off the hook, but he sure got angry whenever my brother goofed up. When mom asked why, he'd say 'Because he's my son!' It bothered her that cute was all he seemed to expect of me."

"How's your relationship with him now?"

"I don't hug him much anymore. I think that hurts him. I'm trying to show more love, but there's so much going on inside of me, there isn't much room for affection."

"How do you think he sees you?"

"You have to understand, Dad's a real concrete person. He is very smart but not an intellectual. Once my brother and I were talking about something, probably Eastern Philosophy, and Dad blasted through the room scowling at us saying we were both full of shit." I laughed. "One time I had a girlfriend over for dinner and he told her, 'I don't understand my children, they're always trying to find themselves, figure out who they are. I've always known who I am, I'm nobody, and they're the son and daughter of nobody!' It wasn't a putdown. He said what he thought. My brother and I always smiled secretly with our eyes to each other, because somehow his sweetness showed the most when he acted bullheaded like that. Plus, he's right a lot of the time."

Journal Entry

We practiced assertiveness in group therapy, but I don't think verbal practice works. If someone doesn't feel they have the right to exist, to take up space, how can they talk assertively, truthfully? It would be a lie, right? I learned assertiveness in dance class. When I started dance last year, I felt uncomfortable making the bodily movements like jumping and leaping because society taught me to be a lady, wear a pretty dress, and mimic the small unimposing movements expected of a woman. When I took an assertiveness class in school, it didn't help, but after a year of dance I spontaneously acted more assertive. I had allowed my body to move through space with boldness, free. I had learned, and physically felt, my right to exist in space. What good is practicing the right words if the body doesn't believe them?

Chapter 7

Two weeks had passed and I was growing stronger. The safety of the hospital kept the world out, so I could concentrate on a plan to escape the Nothingness. Once again I found myself going over my young past, looking for clues with Dr. Randall.

"My brother Jim never acted jealous of me. He looked after me. We never fought much. I remember Mom, when I was maybe five, jerking my arm and yelling at me 'How can you stand here and let your Dad spank your brother like that? I know you did this!' I did draw the stars on the wall, but I just looked at her. I was the artist of the family, my brother the martyr." I grinned at what a butt I had been.

"At age three, my brother worried about the Korean soldiers, but at the same age, I told Dad to shut the door himself, I was too busy. Jim allowed things to happen, I made things happen. Now that I understand his gentleness better, we've become very close."

"Do you feel good about your place in the family?"

"Yes, well, not completely. They expect a lot from me. I think they're angry because I'm not getting it together. Jim says I'm talented and smart, so what's my problem?"

I looked down at my lap. "What can I say to that? He's right. I should be doing something with my life." I pushed my bangs back out of my eyes. "Outwardly they pretend nothing is wrong. We don't talk about it. It's like it's there, but not there. Each time I have a depression, I apologize, giving them reasons why it happened and how it's going to be different." I laughed sarcastically. "Like

I'd solved something! They say they understand, but how can they when I don't? I don't know, maybe they do understand, maybe they don't feel angry, maybe I'm paranoid! I still feel guilty." I shrugged and sighed, "I think my parents feel guilty too. You know, if their kid is nuts, it must be their fault. I hate it. I hate the guilt!"

The doctor's hand gently touched mine. "I don't know how they feel, but I know you don't need to carry any guilt." We sat in silence for a moment. "Tell me about your marriage and the reason for the divorce."

"It was a mini-marriage. It didn't last long. Marriage and the Nothingness aren't compatible. I need to fight this thing alone. It takes all my strength and attention."

Journal Entry
Every day there is a new mirror to look into and see that I am invisible.

Chapter 8

"I'd like to see my chart," I told Dr. Randall. "I have a legal right to know what you write about me." I sat on the bed with my best business-like look.

"I don't recommend it. You know a diagnosis is necessary but it's just a label. It really doesn't mean much."

"I still want to see it."

"All right, but we'll read it together, so I can answer any questions you might have."

Dr. Randall sat next to me, handed me the chart, and pointed to the diagnosis. "Pseudo Neurotic Schizophrenic with Bipolar Affect."

"What's that supposed to mean? " I looked puzzled. "You think I'm a Schizophrenic?"

"Not exactly, but I think you've had a few psychotic breaks."

"What breaks? You mean my chicken eating contest, don't you? In some cultures I'd be considered a mystic!"

"Calm down, it's only a label. I'm referring to the times you lost feeling in parts of your body. The label doesn't change anything, remember?"

"Well, it would matter to you if it were your label." I poked my finger at the typed words. "This is my label! OK, OK." I took a deep breath, "I won't worry about the label, but I don't understand what it has to do with my depressions. Isn't that what this is supposed to be about?"

"Yes, that is what bipolar affect means. You have premenstrual mood-swings. That is why I have decided to start you on lithium. It's not a drug, in fact it is a natural salt already present in your body. Research has shown it is helpful in cases like yours. Will you go along with me on this?"

"I don't care. What's it matter. I'm more confused than ever." I should have left the chart alone. "Pseudo Neurotic. Does that mean I'm a fake neurotic?" My shoulders dropped into a slump. "I can't do anything right, not even neurosis!"

It was the day of the hospital Christmas party and the day of my release. After a month in the hospital, I felt some progress. In the safe and controlled environment of the hospital, I had become a leader among the depressed women and my creativity bubbled over. In preparation for the party, I had painted a backdrop for the talent show, written and directed a skit, written a song to sing with my guitar, and perfected my impersonations of vegetables. The Nothingness had loosened its grip on me.

Wandering around the group of people, I looked for Barry. Though an outpatient, he usually came for the Friday afternoon parties each week. I wanted to say good-bye, to tell him we could both make it in this world. Until now, I had been too immersed in myself to act a friend to him. I found Greg, the student aide, and asked if he'd seen Barry. Greg asked me to come into the office. He closed the door softly and turned around slowly.

"Barry's tried suicide again, hasn't he?" I asked nervously.

"Yes, Sheri. However this time he succeeded."

Reality hit. Everything in the room receded into unimportance. I never got the chance to tell him I understood his pain.

Greg, caught between his profession and his heart, suggested I return to the party, but his eyes said he'd understand if I didn't.

I looked out of the office window into the larger room. My parents had arrived and they were smiling, because after the party we would go home and this would end. But it was not over. I thought

I had freed myself, but the Nothingness had the final laugh. How could I be happy when I now knew that the Nothingness could kill?

Chapter 9

On Christmas day I stood in front of the decorated tree at my parents' new home, examining familiar ornaments collected over the years, some older than me. They reminded me of the magic I had lost. I searched inside for those feelings of joy but found nothing. I belonged to the Nothingness, not the world.

Mom and Dad had lived in their camping trailer until two weeks ago, when Dad had finished the basement where they would live until he completed the house. Dad had built a small kitchen and installed a pot-bellied stove. There was only a bucket out on the deck for a toilet. I admired my parents roughing it while building their dream home but for me it felt like a hassle. Lithium had a diuretic effect, so I spent a lot of time on that cold bucket, looking at the stars.

In May, a woman who had babysat me when I was a child called my Mom. She wanted to offer me a graphics position for the school district. I accepted the job, moved into a rundown studio with a cracked skylight, took my medication, and had a lithium blood test once a month. I skimmed through a few relationships with men until I met Mike. My parents loved him too. He had the face of an ugly frog but the charm of a prince. He also secretly had a few other fiancées. I broke up with him, but not before I had broken two phones on my apartment wall. When I took the second phone into the phone store, I flushed with embarrassment because the same guy waited on me both times. He said, "Sure don't make phones like they used to, huh?" It was obvious the phones had met with foul play but he gave me a new one again anyway.

At that point I decided I had to take charge of my life. Dr. Randall had told me to be compassionate with myself; however, that didn't seem to work. So, I needed to treat myself harder.

I had taken medication for one year and even though I functioned at work, I felt like I lived inside a frosted beer mug. The medication kept the Nothingness from devouring me, but not from holding and savoring me in its mouth.

The counselor I saw each month after my blood test didn't think medication was the answer for me. Of course, he was a smoking, overweight, weight-loss and smoking-cessation counselor. So, I should have known.

That night I took the two medicine vials from the mirrored cabinet and leaned against the wall to feel close to something. I thought about my life. I needed to face life straight on! My friends and family told me I needed more diversions like TV, and not to read and think so much. I walked in a circle around the bathroom, catching only a glimpse of myself in the mirror. On the one hand, I had determination, but on the other hand, I had no plan. Frustrated, my circular path came to a halt when I concluded my situation was impossible. Still, I had to do something—make a start in some direction.

I pulled off the bottle caps and threw hundreds of pills into the toilet, bleeding red and blue as they swirled out of my life. I dropped the toilet seat and sat heavily. With head cupped in hands, I thought, "Now, all I need is luck."

Acknowledgment

SPOKANE, WASHINGTON
1984
AGE 34

"Ultimately, happiness comes down to choosing between the discomfort of becoming aware of your mental afflictions and the discomfort of being ruled by them."
— Yongey Mingyur Rinpoche, *Buddha's Brain*

Chapter 10

During the summer of 1984, I spent my days lying in the hot sun, distraught, thinking, trying to make sense of a mystery. Michael, the latest man in my life, had suddenly started avoiding me. He was a mystery from the first time we'd met on a blind date, a ski trip to Mount Spokane. I remembered how his black hair and beard had contrasted against the white Spokane winter, and though his childhood grief had carved and molded his adult face with eyes that drooped in sadness, his touch had transmitted a calm strength, like a blessing. My constantly churning emotions craved his calm.

At first a mutual attraction, like static cling, had happened between us, but after two months Michael said, "You make my mind tired." I don't know why, but I had thrown every thought and feeling that surfaced in my mind at him immediately, as if throwing snowballs that threatened to melt. I had followed, demanded, and pushed as he avoided me more and more.

It amazed me how many romantic defeats I had suffered and still I marched into new territory like a wound-up toy soldier unable to look back or stop myself. Mysterious men attracted me. Like a premenstrual woman looking at chocolate, I couldn't resist. As with all good mysteries, there was a problem to solve. The men in my life all toted wounded hearts.

There was the Vietnam vet who became a SWAT team cop after the war because he believed himself good for nothing else. He had grown up as a military brat in Europe, living with his mother while his father did whatever military men do. So what did a health educator see in a man who carried a gun, even on a date? His deeply wounded soul exhilarated me.

I had wanted to save others: the millionaire with a drug problem, a sociopath, the guitar player in a rock and roll band, the transcendental meditation instructor, the exercise addict—I could go on, but I won't.

I knew from past experience that my analyzing never solved a thing. It was only a nervous habit. Nine years had passed since my hospitalization in Oregon for depression. I still tried to handle my cyclical depressions without medication, though the Nothingness visited more often and stayed longer. I had moved to Spokane to protect my parents from my pain. Pursuing a master's degree, I thought, made a great cover for my instability. It wouldn't have taken a private eye long to deduce from my college transcripts, however, that the door of my emotional health kept swinging off its hinges. I alternated each term between a 3.9 GPA and incompletes.

I wasn't hiding from work. Actually, no matter whether school or work, I played king of the mountain with the Nothingness and each time I reached the summit I fell. (Or was I pushed?) Anyway, school offered the best way to evade failure because of the flexible schedule. I knew I'd lose any job I'd take, but I believed with perseverance I could eventually finish school.

The sun baked on as I rolled over to give my backside a chance to brown. I thought of an incident in Riverfront Park a few days back. An elderly woman on a park bench had asked to read my palm. I didn't want to act rude, so I gave her my hand.

"You're ill," she said. "You're presently aware of only half of your illness and until you learn about the other half you'll continue to get sick."

It struck me as an odd but interesting comment. True there was a sickness growing inside of me—the Nothingness—but what more could I learn? Another mystery.

Chapter 11

The mellow morning sun filtered through a fan of maple leaves that arched over the path to the Mansion on South Hill, a large house where I was renting a room. A breeze rippled and encircled my skin like a silk slip as I sat deep in thought on the front porch step.

I heard a car door slam and looked up to see Dane, like a freckled farm boy, walking up the pathway. My position on the stairs exaggerated his tallness as he stopped at the edge of the porch and put one foot up on the step. He smiled. "Great day for a hike. Are you ready to go?"

Dane held no mystery. I had met him through a friend and hoped he would lead me out of my obsession with Michael. I realized romantic rebounding resembled a cookie monster changing from chocolate chip to oatmeal. As a desperate love addict, the only way to detach myself from Michael was to attach to another man. Dane had more to offer me intellectually; however, my desire for Michael wasn't rational. So could intellect fill the void left by magic?

I had to find out.

During the hour drive to the lake I pursued the topic of dreams, which I could talk about for hours if allowed.

"Have you ever had a lucid dream? You know the kind where you know you're dreaming?" I didn't wait for a response but started a detailed report of every lucid dream I had ever had. After we reached our destination and started up the hiking trail I continued to talk.

"When I noticed my dream was particularly clear, I decided to compare the locus of consciousness in the dream-state with the locus of consciousness in the waking-state. Now remember I was dreaming at the time. Anyway, my dream-self pictured in my mind my waking-self watering plants in my apartment, just before taking my nap on the couch."

I continued walking and talking without curiosity about Dane's perspective on the subject.

"I woke up from that dream vibrant!" I said with enthusiasm. "That dream-place felt so real! I was afloat in a vast sea that went forever, and my hand had dangled in the warm silky water. I could still feel it when I awoke as if it were just on the other side of an invisible revolving door."

"Interesting," Dane started to comment, but I cut him off.

The sun lost its mellowness and climbed high in the sky. I drew energy from its fire and hiked faster and harder up the steep hill. My mind and body felt fluid, reminding myself of dance.

"Hey wait up!" Dane yelled after me. "We're taking a relaxing hike, remember?"

I slowed my pace, but continued to talk. My monologue moved from dreams to physics and then to religion.

"I think what people want out of religion unfortunately is quick and simple answers to their fears instead of knowledge about reality. The universe is too big for them, but not too big for me!" I kicked a rock as far as I could. As my leg moved through the air, my mind named the muscles my body used.

I loved it when I processed thoughts so fast they stacked up, one layer for conversation and many other layers inside for myself. I handled the different layers as if merging lanes of traffic, moving adeptly from one lane to another without collision. At least, I handled the layers efficiently that day. At times the distance between order and chaos disappeared and my thoughts tossed like salad.

As we walked down the road, three huge horse flies buzzed around my head. One flew down my blouse and I screamed, fanning my shirt to get the beast out.

Dane laughed, "I can see you're a real outdoors person."

"I am," I snapped, "it's just that horse flies, along with snakes and lizards aren't my favorite animals, but I wouldn't kill one just because they're ugly. I can't believe it when people go out of their way to stomp a bug. When I ask why they do it, they say 'because its ugly.' Well, what kind of reason is that? So I ask them, 'would you like to have someone kill you just because they think you're ugly?' That really makes them think!"

As we hiked back to the car, I told Dane about my experience as a TV cameraperson, a graphic artist, and with starting a professional women's resource center.

Dane squeezed in a comment about his love for natural history and his dream to write.

On the drive home we stopped for dinner. Dane smiled at me from behind his hamburger. "You sure talk a lot. It's kind of hard to get a word in."

His comment angered me. People always complained. Either I talked too much or not enough. Why couldn't they accept whatever way I was at the time?

"It's not polite to find character flaws on the first date," I jabbed sarcastically.

"Hey, don't get me wrong, you talk a lot, but you make more sense to me than most people. It's OK, really."

I smiled broadly.

Then Dane added with a comical grin, "Don't you think it's easier to love books than people?"

The next day Dane left for a two-week trip to Alaska, thinking we had become an item. In reality Dane had not won my heart at all.

I still obsessed over Michael.

Journal Entry
We must realize love, and what is only labeled love.

Chapter 12

The morning after the hike I fought to open my eyes. Looking weakly around my bedroom, I tried to coax my consciousness back into the world but my mind kept slipping away. I saw the inanimate objects in the room and felt like one of them. My mind, a turtle in its shell, had retreated. I felt panic, though garbled like bad radio reception. I realized I had to get up before losing all motivation.

Struggling to sit up, I forced deep breaths. A shower would have helped but I couldn't relate. Instead, I left on the t-shirt I'd slept in and pulled on a pair of jeans that were lying on the floor.

My next step demanded strength of will. "I must go somewhere and do something," I thought. A goal, important because I'd have to motivate myself, was a true sign of life. I decided to walk down South Hill to the Sizzler and eat a salad.

Strange to remember, just the day before my desires pumped automatically—in fact inescapably—but at this moment, barely wanting anything took a massive amount of energy. My body didn't always have memory of yesterday's desires. It was very difficult at times to convince my body to act with desire, motivation, or stability when it didn't really remember how. And thoughts—only weak bubbles rising through a sea of resistance, breaking and spreading over my mind like thick mud—they took forever.

Still I had to try.

My body walked with only a vague idea of how to maneuver out of the house into the sun. My illusive consciousness kept slipping and I had to continually goad it into participation. I walked, but not with assurance. Everything reached out for me: walkers, joggers, lovers, trees, and flowers. I walked on. I stopped in front of the restaurant, hesitant to go inside, a cow reluctant to graze, my purpose in life gone. The crowd of people inside appeared as obstacles, irritants buzzing with desires, all revved-up and fully motivated. They repulsed me.

Still, because of the goal, I entered. Standing in the slowly moving wormlike line leading to the source of food, I tried to see the people without prejudice. Look at them Sheri—tap their energy, get involved!

I bought a salad plate and coke, then went to the salad bar and stacked vegetables like tinker toys. Wading through the squealing humanity, I found a chair but three-piece suits sat all around. Were they staring at me? The vegetables were bland hunks of fiber. I ate anyway because of the goal. After gnawing to the bottom of the salad, I could no longer ignore the urge to leave. I tossed my paper plate and cup in the trash and started for the exit. My mind continued its in-and-out communication with the world, and for a moment when my mind left my body unchaperoned, I walked into the large plate glass window, mistaking it for the door.

The pain in my nose snapped my mind back into place but not enough to cause embarrassment. I redirected myself to the door and made it through. I had tried, but my mind would not engage. So I began the walk home. At the streetlights, I stopped. My head felt numb and I was disoriented, as if I was an alien beamed in from another world and had no knowledge of the human street system. I saw lights but I couldn't decode their meaning. I broke and ran across the street, dodging the huge moving objects. Tears streamed down my face.

I continued up the hill toward the Mansion, the trees and leaves glistening through my tears. Only vaguely aware of the buzz of people playing in the hot summer sun, I reached home and hurried up the stairs to my room. I crawled under my heavy quilted comforter to hide. I slept the rest of the day, rolling in a sticky stupor of sweat and depression.

The phone rang.

"Yeah," I said distantly.

"Sheri, this is Jamie. Are you all right?"

I cringed. I had met Jamie a month before. I came home one day and found her sitting with her son on the front steps with their suitcases. Roger, the Mansion owner, had told her they could stay until she found a place for them to live.

They stayed three weeks.

At first, I felt uneasy around her. Jamie seemed to stare without blinking or something. I couldn't figure out what it was that bothered me. Later, she told me she took lithium.

After we had talked though, I found her fairly good company. At thirty-seven she looked twenty, with her long brown hair and impish face. An artist, single mom, and manic-depressive, she said we had a lot in common. "Well, I am an artist," I thought to myself.

She and her son moved into a small elfin house a few blocks away. She called often to check on me.

I reluctantly rolled over and propped myself against the wall to talk. "I'm," it took a second for the next word to show up, "fine."

"Sheri, please call Dr. Bell at Family Medicine. You need to see someone about your depressions. Call, OK? Then let me know so I won't worry."

"Jamie, it's just PMS." I sent my bangs flying with an exhale. "True I'm a blob but what could a doctor do? I'll call, but they don't know what causes PMS and I'm certain they don't have a reliable treatment. But I will call and let you know."

I called, for Jamie's sake more than mine. Dr. Bell answered. I tried to tell him about the depression but words fell from my mouth like chunks of wood. He said he wanted to see me as soon as possible, and made an appointment for the next day at 2:00 p.m.

I phoned Jamie to ease her mind and get her off my back, then rolled over facedown, and slept heavily.

Hours later, I woke with my mind racing. Often my mind came out of its retreat regurgitating all the energy saved while in the Nothingness. I hated it when I couldn't control my thoughts. I preferred becoming a sleeping slug. I picked candy wrappers off the floor. The Nothingness thrived on Snickers candy bars.

Why was I so messed up? But of course, messes were what life had to offer. If you accept life, you accept messes. The key to life was not to get too many messes going at once.

I paced the floor, ruminating over the mess I made of my relationship with Michael. The torture of my thoughts made me grab the phone and call his law office.

"Law Offices," said the woman with a robot voice.

"Is Michael there? This is Sheri." She knew me because I called often. I walked as far as the cord would allow and then walked back. Motion was important. I moved, trying to stay ahead of the Nothingness.

"Sheri, how are you?" Michael's voice always squeaked like a little boy when trying to sound caring.

"Michael, we've got to find answers to why you left me! Why can't you admit you have a fear of intimacy and stop running? We can get you some help. It still can work out, you'll see!"

He interrupted "Sheri, what time of the month is it? Are you PMSing?"

I hung up.

I called back and the robot voice put me through immediately.

"Michael, I'm sorry. I'm scared." "Why can't I leave him alone?" I thought, as I continued, "Please come by, just this once and hold me. I'm so scared. I promise I won't get sexual, I promise!"

"I'll try but I have to meet with my ex-wife tonight on business. I can't promise."

"Thank you. I love you so much, Michael!"

Late that night, Michael stood giggling like a child in the kitchen doorway. His car had broken down a few blocks away. I had just finished the dinner dishes, and my housemates at the Mansion, Roger and Ted, had left for the evening.

"I started to Carlie's like I said, but my car died," he said. "I guess I was supposed to come here tonight."

I quickly grabbed him by the arm and led him up to my room with the intention of coming to some conclusions about our strange relationship. I sat him on the bed.

"Michael, I want you to take a psychological test. All you have to do is draw five things." I hustled around the room to find a pencil and paper.

"I can't draw," he protested flatly.

"It's not a drawing contest." I gave him a magazine with a sheet of paper on it and a pencil, determined to get my way.

"Just draw what I tell you to draw. OK, draw a house." I paced back and forth in front of him.

"Now draw a tree."

Michael methodically drew a tree in the middle of the page. He then drew a sun, a pond, and a snake by my orders. As he begrudgingly completed his task, he handed me the paper.

I smiled knowingly. "I have here the symbolic representation of your psyche Michael, and the key to all your problems."

He frowned.

"The house is your ego, large, isolated and without a door or windows, impossible to enter, or leave for that matter. Anyway, the tree is self-love and yours looks hollow, see?" I pointed to his drawing, rattling the paper in the air. "The sun and pond are your parents and the snake is your sexuality. See your little snake down here in the bottom corner." Shaking my head, "Oh Michael, that's not healthy."

After showing him all the isolated objects in his drawing, I flung the paper in his face, waving it across his nose so he couldn't miss my point.

"You're fragmented! See, Michael, how can you live like this? There's no door in your ego, that's why you can't let me in!"

"So I'm fragmented! So what!" he yelled.

For the first time ever, Michael's voice rose sharply. Now, I'm getting somewhere, I thought.

I grabbed his beard in my hands and drew his face close to mine, shaking his face to emphasize the importance of my discovery.

"Damn it, Michael, you can't go on this way!"

I pushed him down on the bed and climbed onto his chest. "Michael, I love you and I can't stand to see you so alone." With my tears dripping down onto his emotionless face, I didn't know if I cried for the hopeless creature I had pinned beneath me or for myself. "I don't love him because he's a saint," I thought, "but because I'm touched by his struggle."

"Michael, you're alone because you're afraid to accept my love and I'm alone because you're afraid to love. So now we're both alone!" I dropped my body down on top of him, nuzzling as close as possible.

"I don't know what's wrong with me," he said sadly and his arms gently wrapped around me for a moment, then he pushed me away yawning. "I'm tired. Can I sleep here tonight?"

"Yes, yes of course you can!" I started to pull his t-shirt off but he stopped me. "I'm fine. I can sleep in my clothes."

I looked at him questioningly, "Even your shoes?"

"Yeah, I'm fine." He gave me a pinched smile and rolled over.

Unable to sleep, I paced around the room, talking, but Michael didn't even pretend to listen.

"I'm sorry you have to see me so hyper. I can't seem to relax."

"You're fine," he said, "don't worry about it. I'm just tired." He fell asleep.

I kept moving quietly around the room. My thoughts drove me crazy. My whole brain had only a dozen thoughts all pinned on a game-show wheel with some unknown force outside of me spinning the wheel. I had no choice but to accept the thought the pointer landed on. The force spun the wheel again and again and again. It wouldn't stop, and no thought finished before the force spun again. I wanted to capture a thought, if only for a second, to experience it, examine its source, decide its direction, deal with it, but thoughts flew by, compulsive fragments. I felt greatness behind the thoughts, but too fleeting to grasp.

Finally, at dawn I fell asleep. When I awoke a few hours later, Michael was gone.

Chapter 13

I felt calm, perhaps because I had taken three tranquilizers. I stood at the Mansion's kitchen sink making a pasta salad, thinking of how well I was handling the task, but as usual I stood on tenuous ground.

I heard Michael's voice drift in from the front hall. Surely, he didn't come to see me. I hadn't seen Michael since my appointment with Dr. Bell. I felt foolish about my recent behavior and taking medication again.

I dropped the onion and knife into the sink and moved around the kitchen like a carnival-shooting-booth-duck. I didn't want him to see me this way, so I ran up the stairs intending to land on my bed crying uncontrollably.

There was a Xeroxed poem lying on my pillow. I knew instantly that Michael had left it. I read the title, "Kisses aren't promises," and I exploded.

I rushed to gather everything associated with our relationship: a cassette of love songs I had taped for him, a book about marriage he had given me for my birthday, and a cartoon I drew of him as an angel. He could have them all. I pressed them to my chest as my thoughts spiraled.

I found Michael standing by the pool with friends. I didn't know who, I didn't look. I threw the objects at him and yelled, "One authentic conversation, is that too much to ask? My God, Michael, is your mind filled only with Xeroxed poems? How could you?"

His face drained white against his black beard. My thoughts broke into pieces . . . no . . . more . . . pain.

I ran into the house and up the stairs, making it to my room and slamming the door, before I collapsed on the floor. The edges of my lost love felt like razors cutting into my heart. I reached for the tranquilizers on the dresser and a glass of water from that morning. Trying to blink away the tears, I poured the small white pills out onto the floor. No distinct thoughts now, only an urgent blur, but if that urgency could talk it would have said, "How many pills will it take to kill the pain?"

With a remnant of logic left, a stressful day tomorrow, the 5K run, I saved the proper dosage, two pills, for the next day and placed them carefully on the dresser. I swallowed the rest.

"Sheri," a female friend's voice said beyond the door, "Are you all right? Do you need to talk?"

"No," my voice said calmly, "I'll be fine in a few minutes."

I sat back against the bed and waited.

Strangely calm, empty as the vial that had held the pills, I slipped down the stairs and out the back door. I walked to the corner Zip-Trip and bought a six-pack of California Coolers, opened one and shoved the others inside my backpack.

I don't remember much of my hike to Michael's house. The sun was setting as I wandered down the center of the streets, picking my way intuitively. Not a short distance, darkness closed in on me. I continued, mostly in a drugged blackout.

Somehow, I found Michael's house and opened the sliding glass door he always left unlocked. I entered, found him napping with his eight-year old daughter, climbed up on the large antique bed, and curled up next to him.

The pain dead, I could love him again.

I remember movement, . . . talking.

"What's wrong with Sheri, Daddy?"

"She's sick, we've got to take her to the hospital."

Blankness—my senses faded in and out. Sitting up. Walking. Michael's arm around me. Warmth.

I sat on an emergency room exam table. No thoughts, happy. The table, my world. The voices, alien and distant. A small glass of liquid appeared in my hand. A voice from nowhere told me to drink. I drank. Then a big bowl appeared on my lap. Good timing. I retched. Another glass appeared, filled with dark sludge. "Tar," a voice explained, "to absorb the drugs still in your GI track." "Logical," I thought. I drank it slowly. You can't drink tar fast.

"Sheri, you'll need to stay in the hospital for a while."

"Can't. No insurance." I stated matter of fact.

The voice softened. "You need to stay."

I have only one memory from the medical ward, like a white speck on a black shirt—a man, small, standing by my bed, smiling. A European accent, "I'm Dr. Bach, your psychiatrist." He had white hair that sprayed out like Albert Einstein's."

I said, "You're cute."

The next thing I remember, I stood in a cafeteria full of people, I was holding a lunch tray with a grilled cheese sandwich. As I looked out over the room, I recognized the look of immobile faces fastened to bodies that sat stiffly, moving food slowly to their mouths. I was in a psych ward, but I didn't know how I had gotten there. My memory had holes punched in it.

Then someone bumped into me. I moved to one side, still desperately trying to recall if I had come by foot or in a wheelchair.

With reticence, I walked to a table in the far corner. Not an empty one, but the young people sitting there didn't look drugged. I sat next to a blond girl who smiled with wild eyes.

"Hi!" she said, "I'm Lana. I think you're my new roommate. Thank goodness!" She sighed with an audible gush. She leaned toward me whispering, "You never know who they'll put in with you."

I tried to eat but the food hit my stomach like a bowling ball. Lana continued to talk, "What are you in for? You don't look so bad." Her eyes roamed over me looking for flaws.

"I don't know." I realized that sounded pretty stupid, there had to be a reason. "I guess I took some pills."

"Yeah? I tried to kill myself too. I was going to cut my wrist with a piece of glass I found on the street. My darling husband was coaxing me to do it. Then a cop stopped and brought me in." she laughed.

"I wasn't trying to commit suicide," I looked at her with narrow eyes in confusion.

We put our trays up and I followed Lana out of the cafeteria, through the living room, and down a long hallway. She pointed out the small TV lounge. As I entered our room, I saw myself in the mirror over the sink.

"Oh, God!" Hair straggled around a swollen face, shorts rumpled and dirty. "I must have crawled here!"

Sitting down limply on the bed, I tried to think of something to say to my new friend but my mind was empty.

Journal Entry
Do I prefer this pain of search to the pain of having?
Do I prefer this pain of needing love to the pain of sharing love?
Do I prefer this pain of living to the pain of dying?
I must, or wouldn't things be different?

Chapter 14

The next morning I felt wonderful, full of energy, excited about life and ready for anything. But then I always felt cleansed and renewed after starting my period, as if experiencing a new day after an ugly storm. A drop of blood solved a lot.

In fact, I felt so good it was embarrassing. "They'll probably release me today," I thought.

I hadn't slept the night before, but that wasn't unusual for me. At 5:00 a.m. my period started, I got up and paced the halls, eagerly awaiting the 8:00 a.m. exercise class. I stretched and started to jog up and down the hallway, but one of the nurses told me to stop. "You'll wake the other patients."

At 8:00 a.m., the nurse called all the patients into the main living area. No one looked excited about the idea of exercise. Most were still in pajamas. As a part of therapy, a different patient each day would lead the class. That day Ted, suffering from schizophrenia, enthusiastically volunteered. He came to the front of the group, wearing oversized hospital pajamas, his body movement retarded by drugs. "Circle this way," he said turning awkwardly, "now this way."

The other patients modeled his movements, but I stood amazed. I thought I'd seen and tried every kind of aerobic exercise—but psychotic aerobics?

After ten minutes of pseudo exercise, I asked the nurse if I could jog. She said no. I asked why. She said no again.

"Oh well, I'll be out of here in a few hours anyway."

Frustrated, I learned there was no breakfast line slower than one of drugged psychotics. Finally I got my food and sat next to Lana. "Why won't they tell me when I get released?" I asked.

I was looking at Lana, but Ray, a young man with tattoos, blackened teeth, and greasy hair sitting across from us said, "It's the hotel California, you can check out any time you like, but you can never leave."

I decided I liked the guy. In a psych ward you chose your friends by their degree of lucidity.

That night my mind spewed out thoughts. I paced the hall, stopping only for seconds to glance absently out of the window to the alley below.

Why, I wondered, hadn't they released me yet?

Eleven o'clock came and the nurse told me to go to bed. I did, but my body idled like a car at a red light. I needed to move. I took my journal to bed in the ill-lit room, my pencil making scratching sounds.

The night nurse flashed the light in my eyes and I turned away. "Sheri, can't you sleep?"

I rose up and faced the light. "No, my mind won't shut off." I wanted to grab the endless supply of thoughts that surfaced, grab them one by one, squash them, put me out of their misery.

She came in and sat down on the edge of my bed. "Would you like a sleeper?" It was a euphemism for sleeping pill, reminding me of "Soma" in Huxley's *Brave New World*.

"No, last time I was in the hospital I had nightmares from them." I shuddered.

The cherub faced nurse with her halo of light brown hair and whispers in the dark seemed unreal. "Well, you think about it, I'll be back in half an hour." She left me alone.

I lay with eyes closed, trying to relax. My heart raced. I talked to my muscles, "Let go." Then I realized I was terrified. Sleep was death. I felt it lurking, calling me.

The nurse returned, reflecting an unattainable tranquility. I looked at her closely and asked, "Are you afraid to die?"

"No." She sat near me. "Everyone has to come to peace with death. It's part of living."

I believed her. "How did you do it? Are, you religious?"

She rolled the flashlight in her hands. "It doesn't matter how I did it. It will be different for you."

I sighed deeply. "I'm afraid to go to sleep, afraid I won't wake up." I pushed at my fear. I couldn't let go of life any better than I could live it. "Would you bring me a sleeper?"

She smiled, patted my arm and left.

I fell back into the darkness, let it soothe me. I felt afraid but there was a part of me that wanted to die.

Peace. I wanted peace.

I hugged my pillow. "My mother loves me," I thought, and then I pictured my sweet stubborn father snoring, wide-mouthed after insisting we watch his favorite TV program. I couldn't imagine them without me. My brother and I loved them, but we idolized each other. I frowned as I thought of him half a world away in Japan. Our closeness had drifted since his divorce. He had changed, or had I? Whichever, we had parted ways. We still loved each other but life had forced him into becoming a relentless intellectual, and me into a relentless hysteric.

The nurse moved like a night shadow, bringing the sleeper. I took the Dixie cup, feeling on the edge of something. Sleep—unplugging my brain, stopping the wheel of thoughts that raced in my mind—I wanted it. Or would I dream those weird motion pictures shown on cortex walls? I preferred to just slip into an empty space.

Still nothing happened. I didn't sleep a wink.

Chapter 15

The next day I saw Dr. Bach, his face shy but reflective, his hair giving the appearance of moving in a hurry, even when sitting. A grin spread over his face. Sitting with legs crossed, holding a pad and pencil, he waited expectantly.

With determination, I leaned forward to tell him the truth. "I won't go through this again. We solve it this time or I will die."

He twiddled his pencil, making a note. "Why do you think this is so? Would you kill yourself?"

"Yes." I sat back.

Fitting fragile pieces of myself together after each depression exhausted me.

"I'm sure you've read about subatomic particles," I continued. "They have only tendencies to exist. Well, that's me. Everyone else has a life, while I only have 'probabilities' like a damn subatomic particle! Every time I start a new relationship, I cry. You know why? From the very start I know it won't last. Start, stop, start, stop—there is never a middle, no real living."

He nodded. After a thoughtful pause, he said, "Sheri, you have bipolar affective disorder. Do you know what that means?"

"I'm not manic depressive! I get hyper, but not manic. Besides, I went off lithium nine years ago because it didn't help my depressions. That's my problem—the damn depressions!" My heel tapped on the floor, and my hands clasped the top of my head as I rocked ferociously in the chair.

"You were able to hold down a job for two years while on lithium, isn't that true? It was the only time you were able to do that, according to your history here." He thumbed through my chart. "I think an antidepressant might help. Lithium helps even out the highs but isn't always effective with the lows."

Hostility rose, and my jaw tightened. I said nothing.

"You experienced depression before you came to the hospital. You attempted suicide. Now you are progressing into a manic phase. You are not able to sleep and you are growing more and more agitated." He dotted the end of his sentence with a smug smile and raised brow.

"I'm stressed out! You'd be strung out too if you were stuck in a psych ward!" I glared at him. "Bet you've never been trapped in the Hotel California."

Bach smiled coyly. "Patients never like to admit the manic side of the illness. It's usually pleasant, so they don't want it treated. But Sheri, you must give up the highs in order to get rid of the lows. You are bipolar."

"You're wrong."

"I don't think so."

There was a long silence. "You will still have depressions, Sheri, but they will not last as long or go as deep. Your depressions characteristically come on fast and go deep, but you shouldn't have to deal with chronic depression that lasts months or years anymore."

I stood up. "Are you finished?"

"Yes. For now."

I walked out.

After leaving Dr. Bach, I ran to my room and rummaged, fumbling through my purse, looking for my address book. I'll call Jamie, I thought, she's the manic depressive, she can talk some sense into Dr. Bach for me.

I waited impatiently for Jamie to answer her phone. "Hello?"

"Jamie, this is Sheri, I've got a slight problem you can help me with."

"Sheri! How are you? I heard what happened."

"Get this: Dr. Bach, my shrink, thinks I'm manic-depressive! He's putting me on lithium again! You could talk to him, tell him you've known me all summer and I have PMS. He'll listen to you, because you are bipolar."

"But Sheri, I have seen you manic! I never believed you just had PMS. That's why I asked you to call the doctor. Listen to your doctor and do exactly what he tells you to do."

"Manic? When?"

"Remember when I invited you to dinner? You talked so fast at first, I couldn't keep up and you didn't make much sense. Then later you sat at the table not saying a word. The shift in mood was spooky. Suddenly you asked where you could lie down. Without any explanation, you slept the rest of the evening on my couch. Do you remember that evening? Doesn't that seem odd to you?"

I sighed, "Yeah." I reviewed the memory and realized for the first time how rude I had acted. "God, how many other times have I acted weird and not realized it?" I filled up with shame, then my heart turned to dust and crumbled. "I've got to think."

I hung up and started pacing again. Thoughts and memories collided. "Bipolar," I thought, "is that why I can't sleep? Why I can't control my thoughts, and laugh hysterically at times for no reason?"

I felt the reality beating its way in. I saw images that, for the first time, came together and made a complete picture, a picture that scared me terribly.

I thought back to the winter of 1975 at the University of Oregon. I had dropped out of school because of depression. I had spent weeks walking around the city, often in the rain at night crying, stopping at grocery stores for candy or cream cheese. Then I sat in my dorm room for three weeks while friends brought me food and begged me to get up. But before the depression, something else had happened.

It started with Ken, a professor I wanted to impress, another one of my love obsessions. He said he couldn't date me because I was a student of his. So I changed my major.

He was into global events and I had only my small world.

So I started walking to the library at 5:00 a.m. every morning, to read the *Chicago Tribune,* the *New York Times,* and the *Washington Post.*

He finally asked me out, but then rejected me because I had left a brown grocery bag filled with my favorite things—poems I'd written about him, a small stuffed shaggy brown bear, and miscellaneous photographs of me—on his apartment doorstep.

Another wave of shame hit. Why hadn't I seen how weird that was? I saw the depression for what it was, but never let myself look at the whole picture.

Anger flashed with another memory of later that spring. I went to see a counselor for depression. He was nearly bald with long spurts of hair out the sides of his head, and a half-opened paisley shirt. He sat on the corner of his oak desk looking me over. Shrugging, he opened his hairy ring-covered hands and asked, "Have you been getting any?" I ran scared out into the hall.

He shouted down the hall after me, "Hey, you need medication! Come back here! I want you in here Monday morning, you hear me?"

I ran out of the building into the dark street. As I walked in the rain around campus, my arms and legs grew numb. I stomped on the sidewalk, a hysterical war dance, trying to bring the feeling back into my body. Looking around for help, things looked strange and distant, as though thick glass separated me from the world. I was disoriented but still knew my location. I half ran, half stomped to the student health center several blocks away.

Inside I found the elevator, but I couldn't remember how to work it. Sobbing, I walked in circles. Then I felt an arm go around me. I heard a woman's soothing voice and saw a slender hand push the elevator button. She guided me to a nurse. I remembered yelling when the nurse asked what drugs I took. "I'm not on drugs!" I held on tight to the stool because I couldn't feel myself sitting. The nurse gave me a tranquilizer.

I bit my lip remembering not only the depression but what preceded it. That term I had dropped all my academic classes, deciding to take all dance classes instead. I danced all day. At night I'd read three or four books at a time, alternating back and forth, intently taking notes and integrating information. I had felt brilliant.

Was that why I crashed?

I hated admitting it, but I saw the pattern. What goes up must come down.

As I continued to pace the ward, my eyes searched everything. Eye contact did not endure—my eyes couldn't stick to the subject, but wanted information from every object.

"Sheri."

I turned and saw Michael standing with a balloon bouquet, smiling with exhausted eyes. "How are you feeling?" His smile sagged as he stretched his neck in a semicircle.

"Fine," I said, "but you look terrible."

"I ran the marathon yesterday. I finished but passed out at the end."

"Oh, Michael, are you OK?"

Michael shifted in the space around us to get comfortable.

"I was thinking," he said, "if you want, I would go into therapy with you?"

"No," I hesitated. "I'm the one with the problem. You and Jamie are right. I need to do what the doctor says and go on lithium. I'm sorry. You're not the problem. You never were. It's all my fault."

He smiled then stretched his neck again. He nodded and hugged me. I felt empty as a box when he turned and walked away.

Journal Entry: Letter from my Brother, Japan

Dear Sheri,

I love you more than ever. As always it seems that we continue to grow together no matter how far apart we are. I've become a fairly solitary person, away from work that is. Most forms of socializing aren't very attractive to me these days. My perspective seems out of tune with my friends here, in fact just about anyone anywhere except you. We've had lots of different experiences but we always seemed to be looking at the universe through the same pair of eyes. Nothing you say seems strange or alien to me. You are the one person in the world that I feel I could let walk into my psyche without needing to hide anything.

Your letter was anguished but it struck me deeply. It was not depressing as you expected, but gave me a wider hope. You are not alone. I love you absolutely, unwaveringly, and I am with you.

Anyway, you may feel you are somehow flawed as a human being, but I who judge everyone, find you to be the most worthy and desirable of companions. If we had only each other we would have more than most. Whenever you feel lonely, please think of me and take refuge in our very special little community of two.

What I saw in your letter, as desperate as things may have seemed to you, is that you don't have to worry about being enough. You are enough. So just relax and heal.

Do what your doctor orders and remember that to someone who knows you deeply and sees you clearly, you are enough. I have been given many gifts in this life and second to none is that of having you as my sister.

I love you, Jim

P.S. Your whole life with all its struggles, has been a tremendous help to me. Thank you.

Love always, Jim

Chapter 16

"Well, how do you feel today?" Dr. Bach asked.

I had spent the last twenty-four hours thinking about my new reality of having a mental illness. "I feel ashamed at how I acted yesterday. I didn't like the idea of having a textbook mental illness. It's not convenient. People don't like manic-depressives because they think they're crazy. But you're probably right about me."

"Well good. I'm glad you agree. Admitting you need treatment is a big part of the progress. You appear to have two cycles going on simultaneously. First, the bigger cycle of mania coupled with depression, which lasts months at a time; secondly, a premenstrual cycle. When the two cycles overlap there is an even larger reaction, like your suicide attempt. Lithium should help both. I'm starting you on 1200mg a day, 600mg in the morning and 600mg at bedtime. You'll have to stay in the hospital until we reach a therapeutic blood level. That may take a week. I don't want you to get discouraged though, it may take up to three weeks before you feel the real effects emotionally. I am also prescribing an antidepressant for you."

"God, I hate this!"

"Also," he pushed the chart aside, "I wanted to talk with you about elements of your personality. I'm not usually this direct, but you're well educated in psychology." He lit a small cigar. "Do you mind if I smoke?"

"No," I lied, not wanting to appear uncooperative again.

"You realize that bipolar disorder is a genetic physical illness but there are also psychological spinoffs from such a disorder, particularly when left untreated for a long duration, as in your case. I believe you have developed what is called an avoidance personality disorder. Have you read about this particular character disorder?"

"Yes. I've known for a long time that I avoid true intimate involvements. I have relationships mostly out of fear. The ends are never a surprise and I never give myself time to grieve them. Is that what you're getting at?"

"Exactly! I believe you avoid getting close to people because you've learned from the mood swings that your relationships don't last. But now I wonder about my diagnosis. If you agree with me, it probably isn't a personality disorder, as such." He took a moment to think about it and made some notes.

"Well, there is something more," he continued, "You are ambivalent about life. This you must deal with. I knew two people, both clients of mine in Europe, who had the same ambivalence, and they both committed suicide. You must make friends with life, my dear. You must think about life, not death. Find a meaning for your life." He put out his cigar. "Do it or you may not see your thirty-fifth birthday. But now that you have accepted my diagnosis, I feel much more optimistic."

"Well," I responded, "Insight doesn't necessarily lead to change or solve problems. I know I have to change, but I'm still frightened."

"We'll work together on that. It'll work out. You'll see."

"He's like a grasshopper, jumps in and then jumps out."

The skinny woman made half circles in the air with her arms. Martha, an older woman in group therapy, continued to mutter about unfairness in relationships as my turn came to talk about the issue of control in our lives.

"I can't control myself. Relationships are a lost cause for me." I looked at the man next to me to let him know I had said all I had to say.

The counselor pursued my comment. "What can't you control about yourself, Sheri?"

I closed my eyes. "I have mood swings! OK?"

"What could you do to gain control over your moods?"

I opened my eyes in disbelief. My feelings went through the many shades of shame to anger like a chameleon traversing multi-colored fabric.

"Don't you people read charts? First the doctor says I can't control the mood swings without lithium, and then you ask me what I can do to learn control! Why don't you guys get your stories straight?" I started to shake.

"You're pretty upset." Her statement of the obvious angered me even more.

"Yes, I am upset! I'm tired of guilt! Don't you think I want to control the moods? That I haven't tried?" I rocked in my chair, holding my stomach. "Just how do you think you can help me learn control? You're not the expert here on bipolar disorder. I am! You got that. I'm the goddamned expert! I'm the one whose life is chopped liver. What can you possibly know that will help me? Your life is a continuous straight line. You have a job. You're a professional, which means you read books! Big deal! I feel like everyone is playing guessing games with my life while I'm trying to find a way to survive in a world that demands consistency. I can't do it. I can't do consistent! That means NO CONTROL! Not in this world! Not anywhere." I rocked and sobbed with convulsions.

The counselor excused the group, came over and put her arm around me. She sat next to me quietly, knowing not to say anything more. Finally there was silence, except for the squeaking of the chair as I rocked.

Chapter 17

"Have you seen my grandmother?" Linda, a schizophrenic who was both retarded and pregnant, interrupted Steve and I.

Steve chuckled and stole a glance at me with large dark eyes, his black hair cropped short. He spit tobacco into a cup. "No, Linda, I don't know your grandmother. Is she coming for a visit?"

Linda tugged on her maternity blouse. "She's driving."

"Oh, well, I hear she's a reckless driver, better be careful." Steve grinned.

Linda looked surprised. "Did she get in a wreck? Was she hurt?"

Steve laughed. "Nah, she's fine, but you should see the other guy."

Linda nodded vigorously. "Yeah, I can't wait till the other guy gets here." She waddled away, stopping to talk to another patient, "Harvey, are you pulling your hair out?"

"No, Linda," Harvey replied, "it's falling out all by itself."

"Steve," I said quietly, "why do you play games with her? It's cruel."

"She just wants to have a conversation. Don't you think?" he said.

"Yeah, maybe. I feel sorry for her. She's only here until she has her baby, then they'll ship her back to the state hospital, and give the baby away. How much does she understand about the baby? I see her sitting and crying. "That's what makes us human, isn't it? Not our words, but our feelings."

"Yeah, well, I don't know, Sher Bear. Hey, are you ready for your first hike outside the hospital?"

"You bet. I really need a workout." I eagerly retied my running shoe.

"Well, don't get too excited, it's more of a crawl than a walk."

Sharon, the activities director, gathered us together.

There was a light breeze mellowing the sun as Steve and I walked ahead up the hill. I described a book idea we could market called *101 Ways to Natural Suicide*. "The only problem is I can only come up with one really good idea. Listen to this. Eat two-dozen bran muffins and drink a gallon of Perrier. See, the muffins swell and you explode, but there are no harmful chemicals that way." I laughed. "Can you think of any other healthy ways to die?"

Sharon kept calling us back to the group because we walked too fast.

The laughing fits were getting worse. One second I'd be fine, then a hilarity would come bubbling up from inside and I'd laugh until I cried. The previous night, I had to leave the TV room because all the commercials seemed so wacky. Then at dinner I cut my baked potato in half and pushed it open. Thinking it looked like the lobes of my brain, I cracked up laughing again.

"Steve, look at the bird condos! Wow, even birds are buying them." I kept laughing, though I felt scared and doomed inside.

Lana came over to us and pointed to Ray as he wandered off course. Steve yelled at him, "Hey, Ray, wait up." We hurried to catch him.

"I ain't supposed to see things that ain't here!" He kept repeating himself and looked frightened. "I ain't supposed to see none of this stuff." He kept pointing at the air.

"Come on, Ray, we'd better get you back to the nurse so she can adjust your meds. You'll be all right."

"They keep messin' with my meds. Give me this one, then take it away and give me somethin' else. I'm a damned guinea pig!"

"They just want to find the right drug combination, that's all," I said, trying to comfort him. "You'll feel better soon. It takes time, that's all."

Acknowledgment

As we walked back, Ray kept muttering about things floating around us. I kept looking around to see if I saw anything odd, and was glad I just saw the sunny day.

Chapter 18

Determined to sleep at least three hours, I decided to stay up late and then take a sleeper at 3:00 a.m., hoping I'd sleep until 6:00 am. Steve agreed to stay up and watch TV with me.

We had become close friends even though he drove one of those trucks that took a ladder to climb into, and chewed tobacco. He was a good ten years younger than I. It was cute how his face was always red as if he had just scrubbed it clean.

The broadcast day ended with flying bombers and the American flag waving majestically like some kind of religious ceremony. I punched off the set. "There sure are a lot of things about life I just don't get, like the American bomber fetish," I said as we walked from the room.

"Sleep well, Sher Bear."

A few minutes after 3:00 a.m., I was still awake. I walked to the nurses' station exhausted from my ongoing thoughts and asked for a sleeper. "Sorry, Sheri, no sleepers after 3:00 a.m. It's a rule."

"What rule? No one said anything about that rule! I planned to sleep for three hours tonight! You've got to give me one!"

"I'm sorry if no one told you about the rule, but I can't give you one." She shrugged her narrow shoulders as she continued to write in a chart.

"This is a mistake! Look at my chart, I haven't slept for days!" My voice went up. "Please, if I don't get some sleep I'm going to hallucinate!" I made a begging gesture. "Please!"

"I don't make the rules."

I angrily walked back to my room, afraid to make a scene for fear of ending up in "lock-up." For three hours I fought hysteria. At 6:00 a.m. I lost it and scurried down the hall to have my breakdown at the nurses' station. The nurse tried to calm me as she pushed me toward my room.

"Let's get you back to bed."

"What for? I'll never sleep again if you don't help me. I'm going to hallucinate. I know I am!"

"All right, Sheri, I'll call Dr. Bach. He's usually up by now. I'll try to get a sedative for you. Can you calm down now?"

"No, I don't know how!" I looked around fearfully.

"I'm going to call the doctor. Get into your bed and stay put until I get back." She gave me an irritated look, and then left.

I waited for a few moments, which was tough, and then snuck out and paced around the main room. A woman sitting in the darkened living room looked unreal, like a ghost smoking a cigarette. I walked over to her.

"They won't let me out of here. They won't tell me anything," she said, taking an exaggerated drag off her cigarette.

"Me either. And I can't sleep," I said because I didn't know what to say. "Why don't you ask your doctor when you can leave? Tell them you're scared. They have to tell you something, don't they?" I moved back and forth in front of her trying to avoid the puffs of smoke.

"I'm in Hell," she said as she closed off into a private world. I stood staring at her. She didn't look real.

The nurse brought me a sedative. "I told you to stay in your room."

"That woman," I pointed to the shadowy figure, "she's afraid. Can you help her?"

The nurse nodded absently as she directed me toward my room. I climbed into bed and pulled the covers up to my chin.

"Here take this. The doctor said you can sleep until you wake. You don't have to get up at breakfast call." The nurse smiled briefly and closed the door as she left.

I waited. I drifted. Soft flowing sensation mellowed my body into sleep.

Then someone shook my arm. I lunged at them screaming. "No! No one is to disturb me! Doctor's orders!" I faced a man and woman dressed in lab coats. The woman gave directions to the man while he stuck me in the arm with the needle.

"Very good, Ed," she said smiling.

"Ouch!" I glared at the man. "I can't believe this is happening. Not only do you wake me, which you're not supposed to do, but you're using me to learn on." I climbed out of bed, pushed by them and headed for the nurses' station.

"You promised!"

"What are you doing out of bed again?"

"Why did you let them wake me? The lithium level could have waited."

She turned me around by the arms and walked me back to bed. "I'm sorry, it was a mistake. It's OK now, go back to sleep."

I lay down, the softness returned. I lifted onto a cloud.

Someone shook my arm. "Sheri, it's time to take your lithium."

I squinted at the med nurse. "She promised me," I whispered. I took the pills and turned to the wall. A tear rolled down my cheek. The sedative was gone.

Later Steve burst into the room. "Sher Bear, what's wrong?" he asked with concern. "Why weren't you at breakfast?" He stood looking down on me as I cried. He paced around the room and then suddenly swooped down pulling me into his arms. "You'll be OK!"

I rubbed my swollen eyes and tried to smile. "You're leaving today, aren't you?"

"Yeah, sometime today."

I tried to comb my hair with my fingers. "Promise me you won't go without saying good-bye. No matter where I am, even if I'm sleeping. OK?"

He agreed and left me to try to sleep.

Later, still no sleep. I sat up. To hell with sleep, I thought. I got up, showered, dressed, and went to lunch. I'll sleep someday or hallucinate. So why worry about it?

After lunch, Steve and I hid out in my room. He lay on Lana's bed and I on mine, facing the large picture window that framed the city below. "Main East won't feel the same without you, Steve. I can't handle another day here. Who'll make me laugh when you're gone?" I realized as I said it, my laughing fits were subsiding.

"Calm down, puppy, you'll be all right." Steve rolled over on his side facing me and closed his eyes calmly. "Sher Bear, we're going to beat this thing." He raised himself up on one arm. "I remember one real bad depression. The doctor had tried everything, antidepressants, cognitive therapy, you know, the whole bit. Nothing worked. Then I was on my motorcycle one day. My reflexes weren't quick, you know how that is when you're depressed?"

"Yeah, like you're moving around in mud."

"Right. Well, I saw the car coming, but I couldn't get out of the way in time. I flew off the bike and landed on my head. My helmet split in half."

"Oh, Steve," I sat up, "you might have killed yourself!"

I broke my arms and legs and God only knows what else. The funny part is, I woke up in traction, arms, legs, everything—but my depression was gone. The surgeons didn't know I had fought suicide for a year so it must have seemed strange when the first thing I said was, "Ah yes, this is much better, I feel much better now."

I choked laughing. "You're kidding?"

"Nope, that's exactly what I said. I felt physical pain, but I could handle that. It was such a relief to not feel depressed. I guess I did my own version of shock therapy when I landed on my head. Whatever, it worked."

"God, I bet the doctors thought you were crazy."

"Yeah, or that I loved pain. Good old shock therapy. I had a friend who had the real thing. They thought he was well afterward and turned him loose. He jumped off a bridge and killed himself."

"I get scared thinking about shock therapy. I guess it's better now than it was. They put you out and give you muscle relaxants so you don't break any bones when they hit you with the electricity. But still, it doesn't sound like a good time."

"I don't recommend it, Sher Bear."

"I don't recommend depression either."

"You want to walk down to the cantina for a coke before I leave?"

We walked through the hospital corridors. "Be careful, Sher Bear, don't run into any walls like you did at that restaurant. They'll put you in lock-up."

I slapped him playfully on the arm. We bumped hips like kids as we walked.

"Yeah, Sher Bear, I'm ready to leave, but you're probably stuck here for another month at least." He chuckled.

"No doubt you told the doctors lies to see that they keep me here."

"No, but that's not a bad idea. Haw, you're done now!"

The elevator door opened. I felt ashamed as we walked in among the passengers, thinking everyone would notice our hospital bracelets and figure out we were psych patients. Finally, the door opened at L3.

When we walked into the small room lined with snack machines, I was disappointed to find a group of people wearing suits. I tried to hide my bracelet as I bought my Pepsi. Steve needed change. I watched as he opened the microwave and put his dollar in, closed the door and punched the on button. We both realized what he had done at the same time. He quickly jerked the door open, grabbed his dollar and we hurried out of the room laughing uncontrollably.

"Wait until I tell your doctor you microwave money! You'll never get out of here."

Steve shook his head, still choking from laughter. "I'm not so sure now I'm ready to get out."

"Most everyone out there is wacko anyway, Steve, you'll fit in perfectly." I slapped him on the back and we walked back to the ward in silence.

"Well, Sher Bear, this is it."

I gave him a hug. "I hope you crack up out there, so you have to come back." I blushed and looked down at the floor. "You're the only bright spot in this place."

We hugged again, as though he was taking off to another star system instead of across town. He promised to call and walked out the door. The room turned three shades darker.

Chapter 19

Journal Entry
I recreate myself again and again.
No settled, secure world—constantly rebuilding reality.

The next morning I would eat breakfast alone. Everyone in our clique had left but me. Still not sleeping, my body felt like a porcelain doll. My lithium level was therapeutic, but my mind sure didn't know it yet.

At breakfast, my thoughts raced through all my fears about leaving. Going home? What home? The social worker sounded nice over the phone, said she had found an apartment for me near the hospital. I would have a roof over my head, but not a home. I wanted to bypass all the day-to-day living, the demands clawing at my back, constantly pulling on me. Confusion swirled through me like a hurricane, leaving all my emotions tossed and torn like debris.

Then Michael's face flashed in my mind. I flinched. First desire, then pain. Michael, still a burden that sat on my heart. Other people, well, I struggled under the weight of knowing people would hurt me again.

I sat looking into my cereal bowl, realizing I had tried to drown the Cheerios with my spoon. Only a few Cheerios left, where had they all gone? Confusion hit again. What would happen to me out there? A job? Really? "Hi, I'm a manic-depressive. Would you hire me? I can't promise you anything, like confining my depressions to holidays and weekends, but I'm a real nice person." I didn't want to fail anymore.

I needed a hero. "Is there a scientist out there in a lab coat that will someday cure my illness?" My tears rained down on the last Cheerio. It rocked in the wake, trying to stay afloat. I couldn't stand the anticipation of it sinking. I clenched my spoon and pushed it to the bottom.

It was time for me to leave. In my room, I tied the two surviving balloons Michael had given me on to my backpack. I sat on the bed, watching them dance in the air, tears dripping off my nose. If only he could tell me why he left, then I'd know how to feel. Did he leave me or my illness?

I got up and slung the pack over one shoulder, the balloons intertwined like lovers mocking me.

Dr. Bach stood at the nurses' station signing my release papers. He smiled proudly as he handed me a large vial of lithium.

What's he so damned happy about? Lithium was not a hero.

Joni, the head nurse, escorted me to the door. I was trembling but forced a smile, practicing for the outside world. As we walked the long corridor and took the elevator down to the main floor, I thought about Steve and wondered if he was doing all right.

We passed the admitting desk to the front exit. Joni hugged me, giving a sigh as if I was a newborn baby. "Good luck, honey, you'll do fine." She left me at the door.

I looked out the window, watching the heat waves in the air. I wanted to disappear into a fantasy world, a world where inconsistency won awards. I remembered once, as a child riding with mom in the car, listening to the radio, the news mentioned a suicide. I had turned to her and said, "There are other ways to kill yourself than suicide, you could just go crazy."

Shaking off the memory, I pushed the hospital door open and a blast of hot August air hit me. I wished I could put the Nothingness into a book, shut it, place it on a shelf, and forget it. Go on with a normal life. Normal?

Acknowledgment

I walked away from the hospital across South Hill with the balloons bobbing in the wind and the Nothingness still tucked away
inside of me.

Chapter 20

I soaked in the old-fashioned tub that hunkered down on porcelain paws, running a razor carefully up my leg in a search and destroy mission for every hair. When I peeked closely at my knees, I could see little hairs poking up in a miniature fifties crew cut. They had to go! If I couldn't control the big issues of my life, then the small ones would have to do.

My post-hospital experience had a peculiar feel to it, like a surrealistic painting with dramatic images glaring back at me, demanding I deal with them. I closed my eyes, feeling the strangeness that hovered at the edge of consciousness, while I sank further into the tub. I had bought Ivory soap because it was supposed to float, thinking it would make life easier. It sank. Fishing around the water, I realized it was the little things in life that added up to stress. Giving up the search for the soap, I climbed out of the tub and reached for a towel.

The stiffness radiated from my joints, spreading to the cellular level. Standing was a strain. Wasn't I supposed to feel better after getting out of the hospital? Instead, I felt the accumulation of all the stressors in my life compressed into a tight ball, lodged in my gut.

I tried to eat, but wasn't hungry. I tried to walk, but needed rest. I tried to rest, but felt compelled to move. Every effort I made to act normal felt wrong. If only I could yawn, feel some sign of coming sleep.

Finally I slept. After twenty nights with hardly any sleep, ten nights in the hospital and ten nights after release, I slept in my sleeping bag on the hardwood floor through the night and the next day. I woke with a mud-packed mind unable to think clearly, but I felt relief.

Mom and Dad would arrive soon. I reminded myself of my intention not to tell them the details of my hospitalization. I often confided too much. Too many years in therapy left me a habitual self-discloser.

Once, Mom told me I was the strongest person she knew and that she could never have stood what I went through. I didn't want her to find out how wrong she was. I didn't want her to know my weakness, my failures.

At the sound of a knock and laughter, I opened the door to find my parents looking lovingly familiar. Dad with his thick white wavy hair stood beside Mom, whose petite stature and red bouffant gave her a doll-like appearance. My doubts about their visit vanished. They brought my furniture, but more importantly they brought love. We laughed, hugged, kissed. Dad started hauling in the boxes. Mom filled me in on the hometown gossip, as though nothing had happened to me. They were visiting their little girl. All was well. And it was, except the feeling of a trillion tiny bleeding holes in my heart, but I kept that to myself.

One after the other, Dad piled boxes in my studio apartment. Mom and I unpacked kitchen utensils, baskets, pictures, my weaving supplies, and Doogan, the three-foot stuffed dog I had slept with for years. I hugged my old friend, gently sat him in my rocking chair, and then continued to sort through years of accumulation. Soon I would have the apartment looking like home.

My parents' visit was short but renewing. I kissed them good-bye and then continued unpacking.

As days passed, I aimlessly moved boxes from one corner of the room to another. When Jamie and Steve came by, I made excuses to not invite them in. I sat for a while, slept for a while, and then all I did was sleep.

After sleeping most of a week, I called my new medical welfare doctor. "I'll call in a different antidepressant," she said, "But don't feel discouraged. Often patients try two or three different antidepressants before finding the one that works for them. We'll see how you feel next week at your appointment."

I bundled up and walked over ice-paved sidewalks to the pharmacy, stopping on the way back to buy a half-gallon of ice cream.

When I got home, I sat, I ate, I cried.

As the tendrils of depression wrapped around me, I wondered if everyone was confused about life. Did they run around doing their errands with a real sense of importance, or was it just a cover for the Nothingness? Was I more honest or just weaker?

I would sit as though saying, "I'm not budging until someone tells me what the hell is going on."

So I sat.

The darkening of my senses became more aggressive and it bled into my mind, causing distortions. I couldn't control or organize my thoughts into anything meaningful—thoughts folded, turned inside out. Shapes blinked off and on in my mind, my thoughts came in slower and slower waves, fainter and fainter until they became a whisper, threatening to disappear altogether, leaving me blank.

The objects of the external world remained, but at a distance, while my focus turned inward. The civilized world faded, and I turned into a more primitive self, the growling self-murderer lurking within. Wordless voices told me to accept the fear. I felt an ominous sensation, nothing measurable, but there just the same. Tightening my eyes, my jaws, my temples, inevitably, the outer world left me, as though it dissolved. I no longer felt connected with anything. My eyes registered the external world, but only a world painted on a backdrop. I floated separate in a slow, dark, and fearsome place.

No time. Endless.

After a few weeks, the antidepressant started to work. As if a drawbridge was closing across my mind, I reconnected with the outside world. Subtly at first, I sensed objects, the air closing around me, touching me, growing and smothering me again with reality. I moved back and forth between two worlds—one reality, one delusion—often confused as to which was the real one. It left me with a feeling of awful anticipation.

My thoughts started to hold meaning. One would think practice could make escape from the Nothingness easier, that I could just retrace my psychic footsteps to freedom. But each trip separated me from reality, losing touch with the fact that there was a beginning and an end. Maps belong to a place in reality—not the placeless.

How could I be a manic-depressive and human too? How could I fail and succeed at the same time? No more kidding myself—instability, like a termite, had eaten permanent holes in my life-structure. Hopefully medication could fill in some of the gaps. How many depressions were allotted me? How many could I go through and still survive? I desperately wanted to finish an uninterrupted project, though something cold and unrelenting stalked me, making me hurry through things before a depression gobbled me up again.

I would sit in a trance for hours, rocking back and forth with music soothing, hoping to reenter the living world. Death still tried to seduce me with a vision of peace.

Uncontrollable urges—who could I trust with my life if not myself?

Once, life challenged me to learn about people and their dreams. Now, those dreams appeared hollow, the faces of the people devalued—a vacuum filled with illusions of substance, nothing of consequence. Why struggle? For lovers who never stayed, a home never known, a job I couldn't keep. I wanted to scream in rage, but who could I blame but myself for my empty life?

Tired, I didn't want to fill out any more medical forms. It all had to end.

August's hospitalization had changed things, as though someone rearranged my view of the world, as if beliefs were furniture. I couldn't find anything.

Trapped in a darkened mental cube, searching the walls with my fingertips, trying to find a passage out, I felt my limits and they frustrated me. I believed in vastly more than my cubical permitted.

The doctor had ripped away the denial that had cushioned my life from overwhelming grief. My belief that each depression was the last one was gone. I could feel the edges of the cube, sense the freedom beyond, but I remained helpless.

As the medication seeped into my brain, giving chemical support, my life brightened. After three weeks of fighting the urge to sit, I finished arranging my apartment. My newly installed phone rang.

Dane wanted to see me. I agreed. No strong reaction, just minor irritation that people would enter my life again and disturb what peace I had found.

An hour later, Dane knocked at the door. I hesitated to open the floodgates by letting the first person in. I would open the door, but I wouldn't pretend by smiling.

"How are you feeling?" Dane asked apprehensively as he inched his way inside the partially opened door.

"OK." I turned my back to him and walked to the living room, expecting that he would follow without verbal invitation.

He sat on the couch. I sat in my rocker.

"The place looks great! Your artistic talent really shows. It must feel good to get settled in your new home." His freckled face smiled.

"Yeah, I guess. I've moved so many times because of circumstances like this. Now a new beginning feels more like the start of another ending. I'm tired of it." I rocked back and forth, avoiding his eyes. I couldn't do small talk with him. If he wanted anything to do with me, he would have to put up with the grim truth. I had nothing else.

"I'm sorry to hear that. You look kind of down. Are you seeing a doctor?"

"Yeah, Mental Health assigned me a doctor. She gave me another antidepressant. I still have suicidal urges though—really strong ones!" I sat in silence, feeling the drama of my words. An unseen emotion lurked in the sidelines, preparing to jump out and kill me. I felt foreboding.

"That must be scary, but it's just depression." Dane tried to console me.

"Maybe, but it doesn't change the danger I feel. What if I did kill myself? I would have made a conscious choice, so wouldn't that make me morally responsible? I mean, in religion they say suicide is a mortal sin and you go to hell. I'm no authority on morality, maybe suicide is an unforgivable sin. I've gone to hell enough times to see the possibility of an eternal hell. But if I killed myself in a state of confusion, wouldn't that count as an insane act? Isn't there an insanity clause in God's laws?" I clinched my fist. "I fear death but I fear the consequences even more. What if someone who kills herself, ends up in a depression forever?" My respiration picked up. Barely making out Dane's face through my tears I continued to look at him hoping he'd have an answer. If he wanted my friendship, he had better have an answer.

"I don't know what to say." He shrugged.

I thought for a while. "You know that book you loaned me before all this happened? *The Moviegoer* by Walker Percy?" He nodded. "The girl Kate, I'm sure she had bipolar disorder and tried to figure it out. She said it really well—how I feel." I jumped up and grabbed the book off the shelf, turning to the dog-eared page. I read to Dane.

Do you think it is possible for a person to make a single mistake—not do something wrong, you understand, but make a miscalculation and ruin his life?

Why not?

I mean after all, couldn't a person be miserable because he got one thing wrong and never learned otherwise—because the thing he got wrong was of such a nature that he could not be told because the telling itself got it wrong—just like if you had landed on Mars and therefore had no way of knowing that a Martian is mortally offended by a question and so every time you asked what was wrong, it only grew worse for you?

I put the book down, feeling stronger after reading something that described my predicament so clearly. If just one person could understand, even a fictional character, maybe I could win my freedom.

"Yeah, I think I see what you mean," he said. "Life doesn't want to give you any answers."

"I'm sorry I'm so negative, Dane, but it's just I'm not feeling very strong right now. I don't know what I feel. Depression is part of it, but also anger over this whole situation. What's the use in regaining hope if I'll lose it again? The disappointment in losing my health again is beyond tolerance."

I sat for a moment feeling uncomfortable with my confessions. "Why do you sit here and listen to all of this? What's in it for you?"

"Because you matter to me," he confided. "I'm a loner, and I haven't connected with many people, particularly women. I felt we connected before you got hospitalized. I don't want to lose that. I know you don't want my friendship right now, but I'm hoping later you will when you're feeling better."

I looked away in embarrassment. He was right, I didn't want his friendship. He needed something from me, and I had nothing. I let people down just by being me. More guilt heaped on the pile.

"I don't mean to sound rude," I wiped away a tear, "but I feel really tired. Could you go now?" My body stiffened under the responsibility of dealing with another human being. He had needs and feelings, but I had to breathe. Staying alive took all my energy. I couldn't help him.

I got up, leading the way to the door, where we stood awkwardly. He faced me. I turned slightly away, pulling the door open, and then stood back for him to leave. He hesitated as if to reach out to me but then walked outside and turned to look back.

"If you feel suicidal, will you call me?" he asked, his face lined with concern.

"Yes." I fidgeted with the doorknob, eyeing it with discontent. "There's not a good lock on this door. Anyone could break in and kill me. I need to do something about this."

Dane looked perplexed as he shifted his weight. "You're fine. Call me if you need anything. Can I call you again in a few days? Maybe we could see a movie? You should get out."

"Yeah," I said blankly.

Closing the door and locking it, I ran my hands over the wood, noticing how thin it was and how easily someone could break the door down. I sat in my rocker and tried to listen to music, but all I could think about was how unsafe I felt, with that flimsy door the only thing separating me from a potential murderer.

I turned up the music to block out the street noises. My stomach felt open to the air, vulnerable to injury. Images of stomach wounds kept appearing in my mind as I fought to stay awake by concentrating on the lyrics from the radio. Holding a pillow tightly over my stomach, I rocked for hours. Finally, I decided I had to go to bed. I pulled out the hide-a-bed, changed into my nightgown, washed my face, plucked my eyebrows, took my medications, anything to avoid going to bed. I pulled Doogan, my stuffed dog, from the closet, climbed into bed, and held my breath as I turned off the light. I moved uncomfortably under the sheets and settled into the fetal position. I pressed Doogan's head over my ear, wrapped my arms and legs around his three-foot body, and pulled the blankets over my head, curling up into the smallest ball possible. I wanted to disappear. No one could kill me if I wasn't there. My body tight with fear, I tried to stop the images of knives gashing me.

I quickly jumped up and turned the lights on, believing something evil was sure to happen any second. I ran to the bathroom to check the tiny window, then to the kitchen to check the door. I propped a broom against the door so if someone opened it I would hear the broom drop. Then it occurred to me to build an elaborate booby trap. I spread things over the floor so anyone entering would trip and fall: pillows from the couch, my guitar, anything I could find. Wishing I had mace, I put my hairspray next to the bed to spray in the attacker's eyes. I worked feverishly to make my apartment an obstacle course any killer would regret walking into. I went to bed again and passed out from exhaustion, but the dreadful images of violence followed me into sleep.

My ruminating about the night dangers continued for weeks. It seemed to help me sleep at night to go through the consuming ritual of setting up the booby trap, but I never felt safe.

The next week I attended my first bipolar support group at the Mental Health Clinic. The counselor opened the first session with a question.

"How many of you have hit a cop?"

Everyone raised a hand except me.

I started to cry, a hopeless outcast even there.

My winter alternated between walking through the snow to the Mental Health Clinic for weekly individual counseling sessions, support group, movies with Dane, seeing Jamie occasionally, and sitting in my rocker listening to music with a pillow over my stomach and writing poetry. Steve called every two weeks when he passed through Spokane driving a truck. Michael had a girlfriend and planned to marry in May.

During the long chilling winter, I waited for a medical release from my doctor. Then I would move back to Oregon, live with my parents, and start over again.

Acceptance

ROSEBURG, OREGON
AND PORTLAND, OREGON
1985–1996
AGES 34–45

*"The world breaks everyone, and afterwards many are
strong at the broken places."*
—Ernest Hemingway, *A Farewell to Arms*

Chapter 21

With cumbersome furry arms resting on the steering wheel and a red furry foot smothering the gas pedal, I wondered, was this how Clark Kent felt living his double life? I pulled the van into the restaurant parking lot, parked, and swiftly pulled on the big yellow chicken head. Big beak, bulging eyes—a respectable job, I told myself, as I climbed out of the van. Clutching the balloon bouquet by the strings, the basket of candy swaying, I waddled, lifting one shaggy foot, then the other. I opened the restaurant door and stepped inside. The door swung shut. I yelped, "My balloons!" As I fought for freedom, the laughing hostess released me.

Half blinded by my beak, I maneuvered through the darkened dining area to find my victim. "Oh, Paaaaaaam, where are you?" A group at a corner table were laughing and pointing at a red-faced woman who tried to hide behind small pale hands. I sang Happy Birthday, placed the balloon bouquet in front of her, turned, careful not to knock anything off the table with my tail, and waddled out.

Surprised by my profession as a chicken at age thirty-six while living with my parents, I had to admit that life had improved.

However bad my starting over appeared, I felt thankful I had a great psychologist who understood my bipolar dilemma. Ben had black hair and beard, a small round stomach, and a musical laugh. Plus he was the only male psychologist that I saw who did not have the four-inch volume, *Female Orgasm*, on his bookshelf. I could not take seriously someone who purchased that book. There is no way anyone could write that much about female orgasms! So why was the book so popular with male counselors?

I can honestly say that my good fortune was finding Ben. He saved my life.

"You seem to think you're damaged goods," Ben said. "Why else would you be so obsessed with your appearance? Do you think you have to trick someone into loving you by showing them a pretty package?"

"Yes, but I know I'm only fooling them for a while, until they open the package and find I'm broken."

"You're not broken, Sheri. You have low self-esteem because you lived with an undiagnosed illness for over a decade. You blamed yourself for failure to hold your life together and that feeling has become a habit."

"I don't think I can change that."

"You can change how you feel about yourself through a commitment of, maybe, a year or two. Rebuilding self-confidence means building up experiences of success. Taking on easy challenges first, then more difficult ones." He paused.

"Are you with me?"

I nodded.

"OK, let's start at the beginning." Ben said, "There are three stages to any chronic illness, whether it's diabetes or bipolar disorder—denial, acknowledgement, and acceptance. First you have to overcome denial."

"I know I have Bipolar Disorder! I don't deny that."

"Intellectually, yes, but you must let go of your belief that you're at fault. Denial isn't even the hardest part. Acceptance is a life-long process."

"I know I still blame myself."

"Exactly," he smiled. "I have a question for you before you leave today. How old do you feel inside?"

I thought for a moment. "I feel about sixteen."

"That's the age I had in mind too. You stopped developing emotionally when the illness surfaced because it took all your energy to deal with the disorder. You will need to have patience and compassion for yourself until you catch up to social maturity."

"I'll try." I smiled uncertainly when I remembered all the times people had grown impatient with me because of my immaturity.

As Ben walked me to the door, he asked if I would invite my parents to the next session. I agreed.

"I am so glad you came today, Mr. and Mrs. Medford." Ben pulled his chair up close to us, forming a tight circle. "Sheri says you're leaving in a few days for a couple of months in Arizona?"

"Yes." Mom smiled while sitting very formally in a self-designed lavender sweatshirt with a large purple embroidered flower. "We're taking our trailer and meeting some friends. It's nice that Sheri can house-sit for us."

"I wanted you to come in before you left for your trip, so I could answer any questions you have about Sheri's illness."

"She's much better," Dad explained. "I've never seen anyone so depressed."

"I wasn't as sick as in Spokane, Dad."

"Still, you were deeply depressed," Ben interjected. "Here, let's look at two of your MMPIs." He pulled a small table into the center of the circle and laid two computer printouts down. "Health professionals give patients a test called an MMPI, to determine the degree and type of illness. As tests go, it's an accurate one. You can see by comparing the graphed results of her test while in the hospital and the one she took last week, how much her depression has lifted. Hopefully, we can bring her anxiety down more. Sheri's illness has two poles: one depression, the other mania. Have you seen her hyper with rapid speech?"

"I don't know, she does have times of high energy," mom explained as she repositioned herself in her chair. "She's never acted really crazy around us though."

"If the manic episode doesn't impair their ability to function at work or socially," Ben explained, "it's called hypomania, a milder degree of mania. The exact cause of the illness is still unknown.

However, we do know there is a biochemical imbalance in the region of the brain called the limbic system, which regulates mood. Chemicals, called neurotransmitters, are used by the nervous system and fluctuate for some unknown reason and cause mood swings."

Mom reached out for my hand. "I never knew how to help!"

"There wasn't anything you could have done to stop Sheri's depressions," Ben said. "She needed medication to balance her chemistry. You are helping her by loving her. She is very lucky to have a supportive family. Many people with this disorder don't have that."

Mom smiled tearfully.

"The fact," Ben stated, "that this disorder is genetic, meaning it runs in families, may cause you as Sheri's parents to feel some guilt in your role in her having the illness." Ben turned to me and took my hand. "You know, Sheri, there were only two possibilities for you: living with bipolar disorder or not having been born. I for one, am glad you're here." He squeezed my hand. "This illness is like any chronic illness—you can learn to live with it."

I glanced at my parents as Dad took Mom's hand. Our eyes brimming with tears, we sat in silence.

Ben sat back in his chair. "I've asked Sheri to take part in group therapy. She's lost self-confidence and needs a safe social environment in which to learn she's lovable and worthwhile. She also needs to learn how to talk about her illness to others. Educating the people she comes into contact with about her illness will help reduce the feelings of shame she experiences. She's a bit reluctant about the group, but I feel it's a necessary step in her healing process. Sheri is aware of the connection between her manic episodes and her depressions. She's highly motivated to prevent further depression and so we are planning to work closely together to monitor her symptoms in order to catch any potential episode early and adjust her medications. So don't worry about her while you're on vacation."

"OK, but I do worry." Mom hugged me tightly.

Chapter 22

In early January, my parents left for Arizona to escape the damp cold of the Oregon winter. I looked forward to two months of privacy, working on my thesis, and reading. My doctor prescribed a less sedative antidepressant, Desipramine, because I still complained about sleeping too much. Less sedated, I expected to enjoy a higher energy level.

At first, I only lost my appetite. Then I slept less and less until I woke after only three hours of sleep. I would get up, sit in Dad's rocker and face the cathedral style wall of windows overlooking the valley and listen to soft rock music in order to slow my thoughts.

I decided to wait a few days before taking Thorazine or calling Ben. I recognized my manic symptoms but thought I could wait the few days until group. Until then I would maintain control, I thought, through willpower.

Two days before group, I received my tax refund. I drove to town to deposit it. On the way, I decided to buy material to make a suit, because I would need one for my master's orals.

I walked through Fabric Land, touching the fabrics, enjoying the textures, drinking in the colors and designs. My creative juices perked up. I found a piece of fabric I loved, then matched it with another. Each piece led to another, until I bought enough material for ten skirts, nine blouses, and two jackets.

Of course, I needed to accessorize! In a consumer frenzy, I stopped at a warehouse sale. I bought half a dozen styles of shoes, all different colors. The belts were only one dollar, so I bought four, along with numerous summer tops, three swimsuits, four leotards, a couple of skirts, and five purses. I also found earrings to match everything.

The cashier appeared apprehensive as I bought. I made three trips to the car with my packages, feeling like an ant carrying away great prizes from a picnic. When I arrived home, I threw the bags into the sewing room and closed the door.

Then I wrote my Thesis.

I didn't just work on it, I wrote it. I had researched premenstrual affective disorder for over a year, procrastinating over the final stage of writing, but that day I felt I could write a masterful paper.

Sitting at my typewriter, I arranged my research papers in order of date, put a piece of paper in the typewriter, and started. First, I typed a list of scientific words and phrases: *treatment efficacy, generated hypotheses, biochemical imbalance underpinnings, etiological theories,* etc. As I wrote my paper I simply substituted scientific rhetoric for normal language. For example, instead of writing "they can't treat it because they don't understand it," I wrote, "without an etiological theory, treatment becomes problematic." And, instead of, "women with PMS are messed up socially," I typed "the inevitability of interpersonal and social complications with a cyclical disorder of this nature are evident." Also, areas in the research I didn't understand I wrote, "the topics of etiology, diagnostic procedure, treatment and drug therapy are beyond the scope of this paper, due to the endocrinological content."

I wrote the paper, front to back, in one sitting, and mailed it without copying or proofing. I figured I'd let my advisor find my errors. I felt wonderful. I had had a very productive day. (As it turned out I received a 3.9 on my Thesis.)

Two days later, with little sleep, I sat in group, my mind racing. I had called Ben that morning, after a skimpy night of sleep. He told me to start Thorazine immediately. Still in group I squirmed in my chair, leg bouncing, trying to not interrupt anyone with my runaway ideas.

The group started with everyone reporting how their week had gone. Sue, a recent divorcee felt confused about her future; Cindy, a teacher, was suicidal and not taking her medications responsibly; Randy, an EMT, told us about the Aids video he viewed at work; Bob, another manic depressive, had trouble at work; and Ron, a computer artist, said what he always said: "I had another great week."

When my turn came, I blurted out my story of the past few days, ". . . and I left the freezer door open so everything defrosted, I left the oven on all night twice, I spent all my tax money on clothes and fabric, and the kicker is, I HATE TO SEW! My mom taught me to sew, against my will I might add. I sewed my first tailored suit during the seventh grade. What a disaster! I wanted to give Mom and Dad some money for rent and I spent it all and then some. I think I'm a bit manic."

Randy shouted, "I knew it!"

"What about Sheri made you think she was manic?" Ben asked.

"She's wearing too much makeup, she's more intense and talkative. She's making me nervous."

Ben turned to me. "Do you feel this description is accurate of your state of mind?"

"Yeah, I'm having a hard time sitting still and letting others talk. Am I manic or hypomanic?"

"Hypomanic is a less intense form of mania. You're still functional, so you could call it hypomanic."

"Well, I took my Thorazine. I can feel the difference, but I waited too long, didn't I?"

"Do you think next time you'll recognize the danger of waiting before starting the Thorazine?"

"Oh yes! I hate taking drugs if I don't have to, but I don't like losing control and spending money like that."

"Did you call your medication psychiatrist, Dr. Murphy?"

"No. I hate to bother him, he's very busy. I thought I'd just tell him when I go to medication group at the hospital."

"Sheri, you need to call him when problems arise. I also want you to call me every morning while you're feeling manic. You need to accept help from health professionals, friends, and family. It's difficult for you to recognize your manic symptoms because they're more psychotic. I think you can learn to catch the signs early and stop the process, though it's not easy because of the nature of the illness. Remember, your perceptions become altered by the chemical imbalance."

"I know what you mean because I felt out of control but at the same time I didn't know I was acting irresponsibly. Like at work, my boss called me this morning and told me a cop called her in the middle of the night after finding the store open with the lights on. I left at the end of my shift without turning off the lights, locking the cash register, or turning off the helium tanks. I just walked out and went home. It feels weird to know I did such a stupid thing. I had to tell her about my illness. I was lucky not to get fired."

"You've also lost a lot of weight," one woman commented. "You look too skinny. Is that part of the illness?"

"I lost fifteen pounds when I started the new antidepressant. I stopped craving candy and cookies, which feels great. I don't know why that happened." I looked to Ben.

"The medication does have a side-effect of anorexia or loss of appetite with some people. It might even have inadvertently brought on the manic episode. Antidepressants are stored in fat cells, and as Sheri lost weight from not eating, the medication was released into the bloodstream at a faster rate. In Sheri's case, possibly the rapid release of the medication caused her episode."

"Everything I ate tasted like cardboard. I have an appetite again, but I still don't crave chocolate like I did."

I continued taking the Thorazine, but like a train at high speed, it took time for me to slow down. For the next week I took advantage of my extra energy and sewed constantly. By the time my parents came home, my closet bulged with new clothes. My weight had stabilized at 102 pounds.

My parents reacted with alarm over my weight loss, but I assured them I felt fine. I sat them down and gave them a fashion show.

Chapter 23

After the last session of group, I invited myself over to Ron's to see his computer art. When I knocked on his apartment door, he answered immediately.

"Hi! Come on in." He smiled his usual enthusiastic childlike smile, his beard hiding most of an embarrassed blush. His charcoal hair fringed in silver and accompanied by a silver beard, along with a rectangular figure, gave him the look of a Koala Bear. The effect so complete, I'm sure I was not the only one who had to fight the urge to hug him. In fact, I started calling him Bear.

I entered the small darkened living room which was overwhelmed by a large oak computer table filled with disk files and program manuals. A couch sat isolated and unused in the corner.

Ron offered me a folding chair next to his computer. He showed demo after demo of the computer's graphic capabilities. Impressed by the artistic possibilities, I fell captive to the incredible world of digital art.

After a few hours he turned the mouse over to me. I drew a woman's face suspended in space. Then Bear and I drew pictures together. I'd draw an object or design, then he'd add something and we continued taking turns until we both agreed the composition stood complete. When I left, it shocked me to find we had created images for over twelve hours.

I learned that the computer had ended his marriage. He had bought the computer and bonded with it. His wife, jealous, gave an ultimatum, "The computer or me!" So Bear packed up the computer and moved out. He admitted he should never have married anyone who was not an artist.

I fell hopelessly in love with that computer. I spent my spare time with Bear at the computer, immersed in another world—one I wished I could live in.

Chapter 24

A new therapy group started in July. I was the only member continuing from the last group. This group, much larger, mostly women, scared me. I felt stupid and incompetent because the group was made up of professional women with careers. Maybe they had problems, but they all worked full-time. They helped society instead of burdening it.

I talked about how I was finishing my master's and would soon have a professional career as well. But, I wondered if I might be lying.

There were only two men, a shy one with an empty face, and a mean looking one with beautiful black curly hair. Neither were the type, I thought, I could become emotional over.

I felt comforted by Marilyn, Ben's co-therapist and wife. Marilyn didn't frighten me the way other women did. Her honest, open personality had a clarity and strength I've rarely seen. She wasn't judgmental and I felt accepted.

At the end of the first group meeting, Marilyn asked us to choose our Triads. A Triad included three people who met outside group, once a week, to talk for an hour and then report back to group the contents of the discussion. I sat quietly while others actively chose. By default, I fell into a Triad with a withdrawn woman and the mean-looking man. I dreaded the first meeting.

I arrived at the Windmill Inn coffee shop at 4:00 p.m. I sat across from the mean one, whose name was Charlie. We ordered coffee while we waited for the withdrawn one. She never showed. Charlie and I continued to meet through the ten weeks of group.

He looked mean until he smiled. His smile erased the pain in his pepper-black eyes and gave me a peek into his heart. His black curls and mustache, along with a slow manner, gave him mystery. *Ah-oh!* I liked watching his graceful Italian hands give life to his stories. He hardly ever spoke in group, but once he became comfortable with me, he told me more than I could emotionally digest about his childhood abuse. At times I thought he was lying, at least I wanted to think so.

The eldest of five children, Charlie felt it his duty to protect his three sisters and brother. Each night in bed, he'd wait, listening intently for the fight to break out between his mother and father, then he would move the children out of the house to a neighbor's, call the police, and struggle with his feelings of shame. He discovered early the help alcohol and drugs offered in pushing the shame down deeper, out of reach. A resourceful child, he built a mental box to hide his shame. What else could he do? His box had a lid that snapped down tight at the first sign of stress—Charlie inside the box, the world outside. That box was the only safe place for a small boy with so big a responsibility in a troubled family.

He also lost a sister to breast cancer, close friends in a car wreck, and his father. Charlie's dad had terminal cancer. He came home from the hospital and sent Charlie's mother and sisters on an errand. Charlie and his brother sat in the living room when the shot exploded. Charlie leaped over the couch and ran to his father's room. His father had knelt in front of a picture of Jesus and shot himself in the head. As Charlie held his father in his arms, he felt something "swoosh" by him, which he believed was his father's spirit leaving his body. Charlie kept the picture of Jesus.

The spring before I met him, Charlie finally quit drugs and alcohol, which is why he started seeing Ben and attending group. He wanted to change his destructive life and act like a responsible and loving father to his five-year-old daughter. But he kept his box.

After the ten weeks of group ended, we continued our friendship. The friendship felt healthy, until I made a big mistake.

I kissed him.

Until that kiss, I had remained detached. I listened to him, I felt close, I enjoyed his company. The kiss, like the pressing of a remote control button, switched the channel to an entirely different drama. He moved into my heart with his charm and his pain. He told me everything about himself, except what he didn't yet know.

He said nothing about keeping the box. But I would learn.

Chapter 25

A few weeks before my master's orals, I refilled my Thorazine prescription because of mild manic symptoms. I took the increased dosage, then more, and more. It still had no effect on my symptoms. I had problems seeing clearly and my judgment was impaired. I drove the wrong way down familiar streets, struggled to order my thoughts, and couldn't continue my studies.

I visited Ben. "I feel so strange!" I told him.

"It's just a stress response. Your orals are only a week away. I wouldn't worry about it, Sheri."

"Are you kidding? If this is a stress response, I don't stand a chance at my orals. It's hard for me to talk, much less think or answer difficult questions."

After leaving Ben's office, I started to drive home. A question about the medication had been nagging at my mind since the last prescription refill. I took a detour and stopped at the pharmacy. I put the last pill from my vial on the counter, a tiny round pink pill, much smaller and a different color than my usual Thorazine.

I said to the pharmacist who had filled my order, "Can you tell me what this pill is by looking at it?"

He picked it up, looked at it. "Sure that's an antidepressant."

Shocked, I said, "But the label says Thorazine." I gave him the vial. "I've been taking this, thinking it was a tranquilizer, trying to stop a manic episode. Can't antidepressants sometimes trigger a manic episode?"

The pharmacist read the label, turned pale, realizing he had made a big mistake.

He looked at me, and I at him. We didn't know what to say to each other.

"Well, I need some Thorazine."

He quickly filled the order, this time with the familiar rust-color pills.

I left, still in a chemical daze.

I called Ben. "I'm glad I responded to my hunch. I usually don't listen to myself. No one ever told me medications could be identified by their color and size, so I didn't say anything to the pharmacist when I noticed the tiny round pills in my refill. I just thought, how cute. But I won't make that mistake again. From now on, I'm going to check with the pharmacist any time my pills change when I get a refill." I shivered. "Somebody could get killed that way!"

Luckily, my mind cleared more each day as the drug flushed from my system. The next week, my parents and I drove with their trailer to Spokane, Washington.

We parked the trailer a few miles from Eastern Washington University in Cheney, Washington, where I had attended graduate school. For three days, Mom and I walked around the campground, while she drilled me on all the muscles and bones of the body. Mom got excited every time she could remember a muscle. "Tricep! I know that one." She pointed to her upper arm. "That's the one that hangs down!"

The morning of orals, I dressed in a black suit and pulled my shoulder length hair back into a low-riding ponytail. My parents waited in the physical education lobby while I took my orals.

The three professors asked questions, but not one on anatomy. After they finished, I waited with my parents. Fifteen minutes later, Dr. Krause came out of the conference room, smiled, and put his hand out to me.

"Congratulations! Come back in, we want to talk with you a minute."

For a moment I stood stunned. After seven years it was finally over. All those years in and out of school, in and out of hospitals, I finally finished my master's. I felt proud to have finished something, it didn't really matter what. Only that I had finished.

Dr. Sampson and Dr. Emery both shook my hand as I sat down. Dr. Krause shook his head and laughed. "Do you know how many people never finish their master's if they leave school for a while? You just kept coming back. That's stubborn."

Dr. Emery interrupted. "The word is not stubborn, it's tenacious." She turned to me, "I was very impressed with your thesis and your orals, Sheri. Congratulations."

After Mom took my pictures with the orals board members, I called Charlie and then my brother Jim, who lived in Klamath Falls with his Japanese wife, Fumiko. Then, my parents and I ate a celebration salmon dinner at a friend's home. My mind played only one thought, over and over. "I finished!"

When I arrived home, Charlie asked me to fly back east with him for Christmas and meet his family. I never felt so good. I finished my master's and had a healthy relationship with a man I loved.

On December 15, 1986, I flew off on the trip to Hell.

The first three days of the trip ran smoothly. His mother, a very attractive Italian woman with graying hair, greeted me openly and warmly, even confiding in me that first night about her abusive marriage. Ah-oh!

Claire, his eldest sister, beautiful with jet black hair, made me feel welcome, though she and her husband fought openly, calling names and shooting insults at each other. I never could figure if their marriage was in trouble, because in between tiffs they laughed and kissed.

Anna, Claire's thirteen-year-old daughter, looked at the floor most of the time, not saying much. She seemed deeply troubled. As the days passed, I grew increasingly uncomfortable with the way the family talked about Anna, calling her stupid and lazy. By the third day I wished I had money to buy two tickets, kidnap her, and fly back to Oregon.

As for Charlie, he had shut down tightly within his dark box.

He avoided interacting with me, except for a few hostile moments. When I looked into his angry eyes, I felt both frantic and afraid.

His mother chided me, "He's always been this way— accept it!" She commented that Charlie and I should not have any more "little talks" or she would send me home early.

"No," I told her, "He hasn't always acted this way. In Oregon, we had a caring relationship." The memory of his eyes softened by love spurred me on. "I can't accept this, I love him."

"Well he loves you too, I'm sure, or why else would he be wasting my money like this?"

For three weeks I endured my fears of falling apart with no one around that cared. What would happen if the Nothingness came while I was in this hostile environment? I increased my Thorazine and took the rest of the trip one moment at a time.

After New Year's, Charlie and I started home. The plane was grounded in Dallas due to ice and snow. We slept on the airport floor. Charlie's hostility seemed to have passed, but he still felt distant. As my fear subsided I realized how much I cared for him. I wanted to get home and let our relationship return to normal. I felt I understood what had happened, why he had reacted like he had. I knew we would talk it out. I felt no anger, only love.

Chapter 26

"It's best to make a clean break," Charlie said over the phone, a week after the trip. "You'd better come and get the things you have here. I'll put them in a bag." Charlie spoke in a monotone, from his box.

When will I ever learn that to give a man all he asks for can only lead to his crushing my heart? How many times can my heart be crushed before dying? An infinite amount of times, I guess.

I knocked on his door.

"Come in."

He sat on his couch with a book of poetry, his feet on the coffee table, and the TV blaring a football game. I stood by the door, silent. As he pointed at the bag near the door, I shook with sobs. Why doesn't he understand that I need to breathe his smile, like I need to breathe air?

Finally, he got up, walked over, and hugged me. "I'm sorry, but this is best."

I left. Charlie shut the door behind me.

Another loss, another trip through the stages of death. I sat in my Bug praying for anger to destroy the love, but I had too much compassion for his life. I wanted to hate him, but I could only hate loving him. Lost love left me feeling deformed.

I hated the words "I love you." When would I learn to leave them alone? The words rolled out during passion, piercing the mind of my lover until he shriveled and disappeared.

What did he think? Did he think I wanted to live with him and have his two personalities drive me mad, or wanted to marry him and sit around on holidays with his toxic mother and put everybody down? He wasn't worth it. My ego struggled to survive. So why did I want him to hold me and tell me everything was fine?

I wiped my tears, started the car, and drove out of the driveway onto the dark country road winding down the mountain. He once said he was hungry for me. What had filled him so full he no longer needed me? How could I be someone important and then nothing at all? I should have told him that he missed the point, that his breath blew back in his face and so he ran away from me! No sense to that at all. So why did I want a man who made such a blunder?

I drove fast. I drove carelessly. I didn't care if I wrecked. I screamed, which surprised me. But the scream came and came and came. It ripped out from my heart. It expressed every loss in my life, this one and the ones I never screamed over. The car skidded on the gravel and dirt, careless of the curves. I didn't feel so alone while my Bug and I screamed together.

A rabbit hopped into the road, I stomped on the brakes, sliding sideways. The car stopped a few feet from the gray rabbit, as it held its frozen pose. I sat shaking, staring at the rabbit sitting in the car lights shaking back at me. The rabbit got his composure first, and hopped off the road, out of the light into the night. Soon, I started the car and drove slowly down the mountain with hardly any emotion. The scream had screamed and left.

After midnight, I drove up to my parent's darkened house and climbed the stairs to my room. I closed the door. I didn't come out, except to use the bathroom, for three days. I wasn't depressed— the medication forced me to keep on with reality. This pain was something else. It wouldn't let me hide in the Nothingness, which I begged to come and numb me. "Nothingness, where are you now?"

I lay in bed and wrote poetry and cried. After a few days, I called Ben and he said what I was feeling was grief. Oh, how raw grief was. Ben came by and took me for a hike up the Columbia Gorge. He also brought chocolate.

I tried to get away from the grief with logic. How could a man snub the love he said was a blessing? He must be crazy, like the world. But now I am sane.

Journal Entry
I have to kill a dream
To do a sort of violence to myself
Like pulling out a splinter
It holds that sense of hesitation.
I have to kill a dream
I'm not a hunter at heart
But a builder, a creator
I have to kill a dream
To let go so other dreams can form
I can do it. (we all learn early)
I must be as skillful at tearing down
As I am at building up
But it feels like dying
It holds that sense of loss
I have to kill a dream
This one
Then get back to life
And being your friend
But it may take awhile
I'm slower at things I don't enjoy.

During my three days of isolation, Mom would come to the door to coax me out.

"Sheri, come eat something."

"Sheri, I'm going to town to buy a baby gift, could you come with me? I need your help. Please!"

I drove with Mom and Dad to town. We bought the baby a red sweater and ate lunch at the Sizzler. I ordered a hamburger, but couldn't eat it.

"Sheri, you have to eat!" Dad spoke with concern and the knowledge he had learned from Mom, that food was love.

I tried to eat, tried to make my parents feel better. I couldn't help them, or eat, or find the Nothingness to save me from this grief.

A week later, I drove to Eugene for an interview at Sacred Heart Hospital, where I was hospitalized in 1975. Would grief show if I wrapped myself in a three-piece suit? I imagined hearing the interviewer say, "I'm sorry, but you're not quite what we're looking for. You see, we need someone who can affect people's lives and you obviously can't."

Actually, the interview went fine.

Afterward, I walked down town to the mall to window shop. I tried to go inside Penny's, but the piped-in music ran me out. The music reached into my wound and squeezed. I learned to avoid music while I grieved, which seemed strange because the Nothingness never minded music.

Journal Entry

There was a man with a tiny curl whose blackness sweetly kissed the nape of his neck. It amazed me how softly twirling it on my fingertip revealed to me the mysteries of God. Then the man left and took the curl. He said good-bye, no explanations. I can live without the man. I can live without his angry soul. But without that curl, how can I survive in this world? The memory of that curl burns its absence into my heart and though I used to pray for love, now I pray every day, "Please don't make me love again!"

The next week, I traveled to Portland for two interviews. It came down to two job choices, one safe (low skill), and one risky (professional position in health). I took the risky one, a four-month temporary position with the county as a health promoter. I knew I might find myself without a job by summer, but the other job, a receptionist position, led me nowhere interesting.

On the first of March, I moved into an old brick security building in northeast Portland. A charming studio, with an old wooden ice box in the kitchen, porcelain pawed tub in the tiny bathroom, and a security phone with the old fashioned corded earpiece. I bought a sleeper couch from the Salvation Army for sixty bucks, painted my dresser and old trunk a warm brown, and hung old black and white photos over a draped, creamy, lace shawl on the living room wall. The walk-in closet was perfect for all my goodwill clothing. It had three clothing poles, but they were one behind the other and I had to dig my way to the clothes in the back. I felt I should tie a rope around my waist so as not to get lost.

I became a professional woman, paid to think, plan, and talk. I ate lunch at the Hilton, attended seminars at the Marriott, and took a one-and-a-half-hour break every afternoon for a workout at my health club one block away from the Portland Building where I worked.

I worked from 7 a.m. to 7 p.m. When I got home, I would eat a frozen dinner and then read science fiction for an hour before going to bed.

I felt powerless those days—love for Charlie rumbling aimlessly inside of me, while he had the power to destroy me with his indifference. The world surrounded me but I had no effect. My love moved nothing.

Sometimes, I would fantasize that he hurt inside too, but I knew if that were true he would have called me. I stopped my fantasies because they always ended with reality slamming up against me—bam!

I worked, read, and slept for almost three months with little difficulty, but somewhere in the third month I sprung a leak and my stamina seeped out. With the approval of my medication nurse, I upped my dose.

"I'm starting to not care about my appearance," I remarked to my RN. "I've stopped wearing makeup and taking time to iron my clothes well. I am just too tired. I don't even read, I just go to bed at 7:30."

We both knew it was depression.

Great, where was the Nothingness when I called for it? It wouldn't help insulate me from the loss of Charlie, but when I had a job I didn't want to lose, it turned up again!

I increased my meds and continued to do my job as consciously as I could, while I hung over the edge of the Nothingness.

One day my boss blew up, "Well, I guess the honeymoon's over!" She described how I would glaze over like I wasn't even there at times and she warned me I wouldn't get the permanent position if I wasn't careful.

I broke down in tears, not from shock, but because of the inevitability.

That angered her even more.

There is no good time to tell your employer about bipolar, but I had to. "My doctor told me not to tell you until I got the permanent position, but you deserve to know the truth about me. I have bipolar disorder. I have struggled with it for years." I took a breath and continued, "The job is great, but I think possibly it's too much for me. Too much stimulation, and I crash. I didn't tell you because I needed this job, because it was temporary, to test my limits."

I looked up at her, "You wouldn't have hired me would you?"

"No you're right about that, I would not have." Her eyes softened, "Though I never would have thought someone with your history could handle this job. It's a demanding job. You did fine, even great, until recently. I got frustrated because it was getting difficult to communicate with you and it seemed you avoided talking with the employees."

"I know. I'm not real comfortable with a leadership role. It drains me. I guess I found one of my limits." I shrugged.

"Yes, and leadership is an important part of the job." She smiled, "I'm glad you told me, I was really getting angry."

"So, now what? I don't think I could do this job permanently, but I'd like to finish the next month as planned. I increased my medications and I am feeling stronger. I hate not finishing things."

She nodded, smiled. I stood up and left her office feeling relieved. I didn't have to try and hide anymore; that would help save energy. I'd have a month to find another job. I'd survive.

By the end of the month, I had the projects I had started completed, the procedure manual, reports written, and everything in place for the new person. I felt proud that they gave me a going-away party. Usually when I left a job there was no party, only me leaving because of illness.

But this time, there was cake, fresh fruit, and sparkling punch. That party meant I had stuck it out and finished the job without letting anybody down. I didn't get sick and disappear like before. I could return to visit. I still had their friendship.

During the first two weeks of July, I was hired to do layout for a grocery store. I had to drive on the freeways, which terrified me. Still, I was happy with the job. I could do page layout in my sleep. Unfortunately, I didn't realize I would have to type advertisement items from a computer printout with columns. I couldn't do it. When I got fired, I took it hard.

Still, I found another job in graphics a few weeks later. Kathy, the owner of the graphics shop, was a graphic artist about my age with a warped and wonderful sense of humor. I laughed often while working there. It was good medicine.

Chapter 27

In late September, Charlie came to Portland for a visit. After numerous letters and phone calls he realized if he didn't visit, I would keep calling and writing.

I opened the blinds to let the sunlight flood my apartment, then checked the mirror for flaws. My hair had grown four inches since I had seen him last January. Loose waves of auburn hair fell around my face, and the extra muscle I had developed on my legs and arms made me look healthy and younger than my thirty-nine years.

I jumped when the buzzer rang, then ran to the security phone.

"It's me. Charlie."

"I'll buzz you in. I'm in apartment eighteen." I hung up the receiver and ran to the hall. Charlie came around the corner, wearing shorts and a black tee shirt. He stopped for a minute, and smiled. I knew then, everything would work out.

"Walk with me to the Seven-Eleven for some Pepsi." I locked the apartment door and we walked out into the sun, hand in hand. We laughed over something, and by the time we got back to my apartment we were happy and relaxed.

"It's so weird, it feels just like when we were first together," Charlie said.

I pretended to strangle him. "I told you nothing had to change."

He looked down and away from my gaze. "Everything got messed up somehow in South Carolina. I didn't know how to fix it. I still don't understand why I changed. I knew I had to fight for my sobriety though." He looked at me, then kissed me.

He left a few hours later to drive back to Roseburg. I would make two visits to Roseburg to visit before he found a job in Portland.

About the same time, Bear moved to Portland for a printing job. It was fun doing art with him again and going to lots of movies. Charlie for love, Bear for art. Everything was turning out great.

After Charlie moved to Portland, our relationship remained intact for a month. One weekend his ex-wife and six-year-old daughter came to visit for a Saturday trip to the zoo.

On Sunday I called. "Are we getting together?"

"They're still here. We're eating, maybe I can call you later tonight. Why don't you go do something."

"OK," I reluctantly agreed.

I called Bear and we watched a couple of movies, science fiction of course. I was distracted all night by fear of losing Charlie again. I just had a feeling.

It was late when I got home, but at least I hadn't sat in my apartment waiting. I had done something for *me,* even if it didn't make me feel better. I kept telling myself I had done the right thing.

The next morning Charlie called, his voice monotone, "Where were you last night when I called?"

"You said to go do something, so Bear and I rented a few movies."

He didn't say anything.

"Charlie?"

"I called at 7:30 and you weren't home."

"I had no idea when, or if, you would call and I needed to get out. Are you coming over?"

"Yeah." Cold as dry ice, he hung up.

I felt excited and started to change my shorts. The phone rang again. It was Charlie.

"I'm not coming over. I need to do my laundry."

"What's wrong? I really want to see you."

"I told you to do something, but I didn't mean for you to go over to some guy's apartment."

"That guy is Bear, you know my artist friend? Bear knows I love you. Don't you trust me?" "That's how I feel. I'm not coming over." He hung up.

His abandonment didn't hurt as much that time. It didn't shock me anyway. I saw the pattern and I knew patterns, like cycles, were tough to break.

Journal Entry

He charms with his smile, stabs with his eyes, clutching the past between his teeth, while blowing solutions into the wind.

If he had died, I could have pretended he waited in another universe.

He just walked away. Someday he will hold someone new, and though it may not feel right to him, he won't understand why.

Chapter 28

I started dating a new man in November. He was a professional in the health field, with two teenage children. He would be reliable, normal. I replaced Charlie's picture with his.

Feeling safe in my new relationship, I stopped by Charlie's house. He looked surprised as he opened the door. I put my finger on his chest, poking with anger, backing him across the room.

"I don't deserve to be treated like this!"

He sat quietly on the couch as I gave him a stern lecture on friendship and love. He listened and agreed. As I started to leave, he rose and said. "You know I love you."

I looked away, shaking my head. "I can't keep going through this."

He nodded and said he understood.

It took me about two months to realize my new relationship with Tim was a dud.

"Where are the normal people?" I wondered. I don't need this on-and-off behavior from Tim. I can get that from Charlie.

So I called Charlie.

"Want to go to a movie?"

"Yes, but don't tease me."

"I'm not teasing you. I want to see you."

We saw a movie, bought a take-home pizza, and baked it.

We lasted through Valentine's Day.

I thought I'd go crazy going through another abandonment. I grabbed my heart and shook it, "FIND A WAY TO STOP THIS!" A flurry of unmarked emotions stormed my body.

Then I found the switch. I turned all my emotions and desires off. *Yeah right!*

I knew if Charlie could do it, I could. I just never wanted to until then. Detachment was a message all the world religions taught, and for good reason. But was I really detached or just suppressing my feelings?

I enjoyed my time alone. It felt solid, reliable. With men, I waited, feeling a certain something might happen, but it never did. Not a solid something, like stark nights alone, knowing exactly what it meant to be alive, not pushing back this thought or that because it might hurt the relationship. I would live alone, with no fantasy salvation by a man's love.

I knew I had depended too much on men, but I was afraid, needing some man to tell me I was enough. At that point, the price had risen too high. I couldn't keep risking and survive. I had to let go.

I knew for every romance I found and lost, a piece of that person stayed in my heart. My heart had grown heavy from love quills. My soul felt like a porcupine!

I had to face the present, let the past go. If I ventured too far into the future, I panicked, but in the present I could function by myself, moving, talking, and doing. My core no longer felt scrambled.

I thought of the dream I had at thirteen, about my life journey on a long jungle path. I had assumed the path was straight, but it occurred to me the path might have circled around. I saw a picture in my mind of the jungle path surrounding a beautiful valley with a peaceful lake. I realized I got off the path by changing my point of view. I had chosen to stay in the jungle. I had grown attached to the passion, willing to risk danger in order to obtain my desire from moment to moment. One small step, one realization, brought detachment.

I would remain in the valley alone, until someone committed to join me there. No more trips into the jungle of romantic passion. I felt the power and miracle of my escape.

Life is not about romantic love.

Chapter 29

I lived through the next four months dipped in calmness. *OK, some of that calmness was from medication.* I smiled in my detachment, knowing tranquility and passion were not roommates, and I had made the proper choice. I enjoyed work. Evenings I read, not just science fiction. Once or twice a week, Bear and I would go to a movie.

I took Bear to dinner on his forty-first birthday. As I ate my hot and sour soup, he started a conversation I didn't expect.

"I had a dream last night. It made me realize I had to start expressing my thoughts to you."

"Oh?" I looked up from my soup.

"I do think about stuff, you know?"

I nodded.

"I have a spiritual side. I just never talk about it. I've read about the religions and know that they're basically the same down deep. The differences are mostly surface stuff because of the cultures and time of their origin. But they all teach unity and give guidelines for living life."

Then he surprised me again by talking about physics and astronomy. For the next week, we continued to talk about science and religion, my favorite topics. It felt wonderful to have someone to talk to about inner beliefs and science.

One night, while talking on the phone with Bear, I asked, "Are we dating now?"

"Ah, I don't know. If you want—I mean we could."

I thought for a moment, "OK, but no kissing until we know more. I lose perspective when I kiss someone. I need to protect myself until I know it's safe. It's hard to see someone's character with fogged-up glasses." I laughed. "I guess that sounds pretty stupid since, in this culture right now, sex is expected. With my new attitude I'll probably end up alone, because men think it's a waste of time and downright foolish to hang around a woman, if there's no sex."

"Well I guess that makes me a fool then."

"What?"

"I've hung around you for three years without sex. I know you and love you and I'm still here."

"I guess that's true," I chuckled. "Not that you're a fool, I mean, but that you're still here."

Chapter 30

One day I was working alone at the print shop, folding cards by hand. I thought about Bear and how he had loved art as a boy, but was discouraged by everyone around him telling him he couldn't make a living with art. Maybe because his father abandoned his family during Bear's teen years, or because Vietnam put his soul in shock, or because his ex-wife was jealous of his computer, he had remained in emotional limbo, never living his own life.

Bear needed what I needed: a companion that understood the creative drive of an artist, freedom to explore his talents, a lifestyle with art and spirituality at its core.

I knew what I had to do.

At the end of the shift, I punched out at the time-clock, wrote some thoughts on a scrap of paper, and put it in my pocket. I called Bear at work.

"Bear, this is Sheri. Can you come by after work, I want to talk to you about an idea I have. I'll fix dinner."

"Sure, it'll be about an hour before I finish work."

I entered my apartment focused on my goal. I cut a cantaloupe in half, filled the halves with strawberries and green grapes, and put them back into the refrigerator. I set the table, cooked the fettuccine, put candles on the table, and slipped into a black lace dress.

As I lit the candles, Bear knocked on the door.

I was ready.

I opened the door and smiled. Bear tried to smile, but his eyes got stuck on my black lace dress. With a bewildered expression he stepped inside, standing awkwardly in his baggy cords and ink stained tee-shirt, looking at my dress.

"Ah, what's up?"

"Fettuccine!" I showed him to the table.

"Oh, well, good."

We sat and ate. I talked about something unimportant while Bear looked at the candles, a bit dazed over what, to him, must have appeared a mystery.

After we ate, I suggested we go to the living room. I sat next to Bear on the couch.

"I worked alone today, so I had all day to think. I have an idea I think would work for both of us." I hesitated nervously, having a hard time remembering everything I had written down. I had wanted this to seem somewhat romantic but I needed accuracy more. "Do you mind if I use my notes? I don't want to skip any important points."

"Whatever," he said shyly.

"OK, just a moment. I wrote everything down." I hurried over to the closet and pulled the folded paper out of my jeans pocket.

"This is embarrassing to use notes, but I'm a bit nervous. Let me preface this with, if you don't like my idea, that's all right. Or if you like it, but need to modify it in some way, that's fine too."

He nodded.

"OK, here goes." I swallowed and straightened my back. "We both want to dedicate ourselves to developing our talent. In the past, we sold out. We gave ourselves away to relationships that brought us down." I checked my list. "Neither of us want a traditional marriage with kids and a big house as our major bond. We need creativity. Creativity is our bond!" I cleared my throat. "We're both in a place now where we either go it alone or we go it together. See what I mean?"

He nodded again.

I looked down at my notes. This was the scary part. "I mean, Bear, that you and I should get married." I kept talking, afraid to let him speak. I intently watched his face for clues of approval or rejection. "A real small wedding with only witnesses, no hassles. Just get into a supportive lifestyle." His lip curled up slightly on one side of his mustache. A smile? I felt a need to explain further. "I'm suggesting marriage because I can't stand another uncommitted boyfriend. With our marriage we would go right to the core of the relationship—art and spirituality."

He nodded again.

"Well what do you think for God's sake?" Bear grinned widely. "Well, actually, I was thinking along the same lines, only maybe not so detailed," he chuckled.

"I know we both said we'd never marry again, but I wouldn't feel afraid of a marriage with you."

"It'd be different, healthy," he said. Happiness broke across his face. "I already love your family too."

"So when should we tell them?"

"We could drive down this weekend."

Late Friday night, we drove up Hi Lo Lane. It was not unusual for Bear to drive me home; his mother lived in a nearby town.

I made up the bed in the basement for him. Mom and Dad were getting ready for bed at 11:00 p.m. Bear and I had planned to tell them the next day together, but as I started up the stairs to my bedroom, I stopped. What if they disapproved, but didn't feel comfortable saying anything in front of Bear? I needed to know how they really felt. Besides, I had become a Bahá'í, and the Bahá'í teachings required that I get my parents' consent to marry.

I knocked at their bedroom door.

"Come on in," Mom's voice said warmly.

I sat on the bed while Mom and Dad took out their contacts at the double sinks in the open bathroom nook.

"I wanted to tell you something. Bear and I have decided to get married."

"I knew it!" Mom said happily. She ran over and threw her arms around me.

"Oh, honey, I'm so happy!" Dad closed his contact case and joined us. "I always wondered why you couldn't marry him, he's so good to you. This is great."

"You don't think it's too impulsive? We don't plan to wait until Jim and Fumiko get back from Japan. We thought we would just get married with witnesses in Portland, no wedding hassles. Then later we'll have a BBQ here. No presents!"

"Whatever makes you two happy," Mom said as she hugged Dad's arm.

The next morning, Bear and I sat drinking coffee when I told him about the conversation with my parents. He seemed relieved. Mom and Dad came out of the bedroom like smiling elves, got their coffee, and then made a lot of fuss over Bear.

"We're so pleased, Ron." Mom gave him a kiss on the cheek and a hug.

"We're happy to have you in our family."

After breakfast, Dad took Bear by the arm. "Let's go to the shop. I want to show you where all my tools are. You know you can use them anytime."

Mom and I snickered as they left the room.

"Isn't that cute," Mom said.

"Yeah, male bonding," I said.

In the next two weeks, I got the flu, Bear cut the end of his finger off, we got the marriage license, bought Hopi Indian wedding rings, and rented an apartment. On July 19, 1989, we got married at 6:00 a.m. at a friend's house with two witnesses. We had banana nut muffins for wedding cake, and left for a two-day camping honeymoon.

After my brother Jim and his wife and two-year-old daughter returned from Japan, my parents gave us a party. I was surprised to find a large carrot cake on a white lace covered table, flowers and decorations lining long tables, and a large pile of wedding gifts.

A woman in blue approached me. "You must be Sheri?" She reached for my hand. "I don't think we have met," she said.

"No I don't believe we have." I tried to smile, "It's a pleasure to meet you."

She handed me a gift and I slipped away to find my mother.

"Mom, I told you specifically to tell people not to bring gifts. This is embarrassing!"

"Well, honey, I did tell them, but they wanted to, so I told them what you needed and in what color."

Chapter 31

I found it interesting how my mind, for so many years, tucked away, transformed, and denied experiences in order to endure my illness. I felt as frightened as an insecure child with every new situation.

Before medication, my family and friends held me up like an external skeleton. I loved them because I needed them. I structured my relationships around my needs, not theirs. I dimly realized somewhere inside my heart that others had needs, but I never could get them in focus while I was busy surviving.

Medication gave me my own skeleton. For the first time I experienced living, instead of just surviving. I could stand on my own.

My view of the world became clearer. I no longer felt submerged underwater, separated from the world as though looking through a fluid. I touched my environment directly. I felt people in my heart like never before, feelings for them bubbling up from the depths and filling my soul with life.

Unfortunately, my first clear view of the world came during the first Gulf War. The reality of human vulnerability to life and death hit like a Scud missile. I cried for days. The real world was wild and unpredictable. My fear of death surfaced again, only this time, not just for my life, but for everyone. Humanity might die. Humanity might commit suicide!

I plunged into my new reality, wide-eyed and trembling in front of the television. The war abraded my heart, leaving it sore and angry. I wanted to scream at people, "Don't you see we are killing ourselves!"

At work I talked to my new friend Bobbie about my feelings while my identity crisis with the world waged on. For about a month, I obsessed over how negative the "normal people" were.

"Bobbie, everyone talks behind everybody's back. I never noticed before because I was so glazed over with my own problems. Their judgments scare me. It seems everyone gets stuck in a category right off the bat: saint, stupid, crazy, or jerk. I've missed out on so much socially, my naiveté must make me look stupid. I hate that. It makes me want to tell everyone I'm crazy. I'd rather be thought of as crazy than as stupid."

Bobbie seemed to enjoy our talks, though at the time, I believed even she thought of me as stupid and strange. I never felt comfortable around anyone.

Then, one day I found insight into a basic truth about people. All my criticism blew away like feathers when I saw to the heart of the matter.

There are no "normal" people.

I realized fear was fear, and if I could live with fear in the Nothingness, I could live with it in the world.

My life was flowing instead of choking and gurgling down the drain. I felt bad about my social immaturities but I could grow. After all, I thought, a personality was not an object like an eggplant or a kazoo, but a loosely organized system of beliefs, thoughts, and behaviors. I could rearrange them into new patterns, suitable patterns.

My illness had affected my nervous system somehow and it was very touchy. The American pace was fast-forward. I tried to keep up. Even with medication, I knew the modern pace would run me right into the Nothingness.

I had to simplify.

I bagged up clothes that required ironing, realizing that to consume was the American way, but I had to lighten my load. Things took energy. I taught myself to savor, not consume.

I started to meditate again. I had tried meditation in 1975, but had adverse reactions: electrical shocks in my chest, and dots of light blinking around my head. Now, on medication, it was worth another chance. So I meditated once per day for twenty minutes. I would drop myself willingly into a placeless state, not unlike the Nothingness, except instead of shadows, I washed myself in light and peace. It felt as though those giant hands outside of time were holding me again. My health expanded like a folded paper fan, a little each month. Most significantly, I could respond to the needs of others. The fear was still there, but it didn't hog all the space in my heart.

I remember the night I realized I had become fully alive in this world. It dawned on me while chopping vegetables for dinner that suicide was no longer an option. Death would take me by surprise like everyone else: a heart attack, earthquake, or old age.

I had cooked lasagna in the microwave and placed it on the dining table. It felt simple and real.

Bear smiled as he dished up a portion on his plate. Unfortunately, the pasta and cheese had coalesced into rubber, and Bear kept trying to eat it.

I pushed my plate back and said, "I'm done."

Pretending to misunderstand me, Bear said without looking up, "No honey, you're not dumb, you're just slow." Then he pushed his plate back as well. "You nuked it too long again, didn't you?" He got up from the table and started toward the kitchen cupboard. "We got any popcorn?"

I grinned. "I guess this means no kiss for the cook?"

"Sure I'll kiss the cook." He planted his lips on the tinted glass of the microwave with a loud smack.

I laughed, and thought to myself, "how great to be silly."

Chapter 32

Our three-year friendship was great; our five-year marriage, not so much. Bear had anger issues that only showed up after I moved in with him. In the fifth year of marriage, I went to the Portland Bahá'í Assembly for advice. They invited Bear in for counseling with me, but he said no. The Assembly suggested I go ahead with a year of patience* and then divorce. So when Bear and I went for coffee one Sunday morning, I told him we needed to go back to just friends. I moved one block away. After I moved out, Bear returned to his old sweet self and we did art and movies together again.

When the year of waiting ended, I took a day off work and drove down town to the courthouse. After going through the metal detector, I found my way to a long line. I wondered if everyone in the line was there for a divorce. It took an hour to reach the clerk's window. I reached into my bag for the paperwork and money as I stepped up to the window. "I'm here for a divorce," I said. "Ninety-seven dollars, right?" A friend had told me this was how much it would cost.

The woman in the window looked at me for a few seconds before explaining, "It costs $250."

---

* According to Bahá'í law, if a married couple wishes to divorce, they are required to live apart for at least one year, during which they must make every effort to reconcile. If at the end of this "year of patience," their differences prove irreconcilable, they are permitted to divorce.

"What, you're kidding! $250?"

She shifted her smirk from one side of her mouth to the other. "Yeah."

"Great!" I scooped up my money, stuffed it into my bag along with the paperwork, and marched out into the street. I didn't want to go back to work, so I climbed into my car and drove to Lloyd Center mall. I wandered the mall until I passed a large sign in a beauty parlor window that said fifty percent off perms. I walked in. A bleached blond guy with orange plaid pants waved me into a seat. As he whipped an apron like a matador around my neck he asked, "So what are you up to this fine day?"

I smiled sweetly, "I went to get a divorce, but couldn't afford it, so I decided to get a perm instead."

Two weeks later a check for $250 arrived in the mail from my parents with a note, "Get a divorce."

One week after the divorce, Charlie and his daughter Sara stood on my doorstep asking me if I wanted to see a movie. *Ah-oh!*

The relationship lasted a whopping two and a half years. We only saw each other on Saturdays or Sundays. He lived in another town.

Then depressive symptoms started; I couldn't remember how to fax, I cried when deciding what to wear. There was a heat wave and I had not slept well in a month. My doctor suggested I go visit my parents in Roseburg because they had an air conditioner, and I could catch up on my sleep. When I got to my folks' house they informed me their air conditioner was on the blink. I stayed a week anyway and then drove back to Portland. During the drive home, I developed a sore throat and a fever. By the time I reached home, I was so weak I lay down on the kitchen floor with the telephone and tried to call Charlie. I spent the night in the fetal position on the kitchen floor, hugging the phone.

Once my flu ran its course, my doctor put me in a psych daycare at OHSU. It lasted about a month, but my depression worsened.

One day, hysterical, I couldn't stop crying, so my doctor put me in the hospital to change my medications and add a mood stabilizer called Depakote. The side-effects were bazaar. It often felt as though a live fish were flopping around in my head, and for some reason I could no longer cry.

I stayed ten days and met many interesting people on the ward. My roommate was psychotic and I would wake up in the middle of the night with her face in mine. She only said one thing, "Got a match?" Then there was my favorite schizophrenic, who stared at me all the time. Finally he said, "I am sorry I stare, but women are like Christmas every day!"

I did hang out with a street kid with a cocaine addiction and bipolar disorder. Our lives were entirely different on the outside, but on the ward we were the best of friends. I remember us watching the alien autopsy together and speculating about its truth.

When the fish in my head calmed down, they sent me home. A week later Charlie called to see how I was doing. I accused him of not calling all week and felt he wasn't acting supportive. He said he had called every night. I said he was lying. Then my mother called and said Lisa, my niece, had called me a few days ago and said I sounded weird. I had no memory about that phone call either, but I trusted my mother's word. It turned out that the Ambien I was taking for sleep was causing amnesia. Oops, Charlie was in his box. No more Charlie.

Three months later, I celebrated Christmas in Roseburg with my parents. I sat opening gifts in my long, blue, flannel gown when the phone rang. "Hi, Sheri, this is Charlie. I am here in Roseburg at a motel. Will you stay with me on Christmas?"

I paused a moment in unbelief. "Why aren't you with Sara and your mother?"

He replied, "You know my mother. I just couldn't take it. And I really need to see you."

"I can't. I came to spend Christmas with my family. You can come over here if you like?"

"OK." A few minutes later, Charlie arrived with a present for my mother, and visited for about an hour and then left. I wanted to go with him but I knew it was the wrong thing to do. Why couldn't Charlie get it right just once?

After Christmas, back in Portland, I woke up with a life-changing thought. "I can love anyone, but I must love the relationship." That really narrowed the field. I called Charlie, who was planning to come over that day, and told him not to. I explained, "Our relationship isn't healthy for either of us. Call if you want to talk, but we can't see each other anymore."

Five months later, I was rooming with Suzie, a secretary at the research institute I worked at. We were packing to move into a house. As she was wrapping a glass in newsprint, she waved the *Willamette Weekly* in my face and said it was time for me to date again. I had always felt interested in the personal ads as a way to meet someone but I was always in a relationship. Still, I wasn't ready to date. I took the *Weekly* and started to read some of the ads out loud. We laughed as I read through them, but one actually interested me. "Spiritually eclectic, vegetarian, athletic, intellectual, classical music, art, cats, movies, hot springs, cycling, dancing, listening."

On impulse, and with Suzie egging me on, I called. There was a tape recording of him talking about himself. Then I recorded a message, "Hi, I am Sheri, a Bahá'í and artist. We have a lot in common, but you seem a bit too smooth. Maybe we could talk before meeting."

"Yeah, like he'll call," said Suzie laughing, "after you insulted him."

But four hours later he called and his name was Bill. We met at a Starbuck's in another neighborhood and talked for hours. He was fresh and fit, with a big white smile. He also had one green eye and one blue.

We saw each other every day. It wasn't long before he said "I love you." And I replied, "You scare me." But we married one year later in a rock garden located on top of a nearby restaurant overlooking the Willamette River.

The only requirement for a Bahá'í marriage is that both parties say, "We will, all, verily abide by the Will of God" in front of witnesses. We followed this with a wedding prayer. Then we all went to breakfast together. I wore a long royal blue silk dress and Bill wore an orange Nero shirt. No flowers, no hassles.

Recovery

"Know thou that the soul of man is exalted above, and is independent of all infirmities of body or mind . . . the soul itself remaineth unaffected by any bodily ailments. Consider the light of the lamp. Though an external object may interfere with its radiance, the light itself continueth to shine with undiminished power."
—Bahá'u'lláh, *Gleanings from the Writings of Bahá'u'lláh,* no. 80.2

Chapter 33

Holding my orange backpack with white knuckles, I walked onto the plane. Bill and I were not able to find a seat together, so there was plenty of time to close my eyes and think about my life. We were flying to Chicago so I could visit the Bahá'í National Center, and Bill could attend a Freedom from Religion 2010 Conference for atheists. What an eclectic trip!

While on the plane, I thought back. Getting engaged to Vance, my high school sweetheart, gave me the courage for a life change. So I had a conversation with Jesus, "I hate going to church. Why do ministers get all the say in the matter of spirit?" I explained to Him that I wanted to take a yearlong sabbatical and search for a spiritual path that wasn't so one-sided. Surely there had to be more than one way to look at existence? Ritual and organ music just weren't my way.

During that year at the University of Oregon, I learned about civil rights movements. I also found out for the first time that more than one religion existed. But I found no path that pleased my view of things. It looked like I was going to have to go back to church as I had promised. Vance and I picked a big fancy church and attended. About thirty minutes into the sermon, we looked at each other and walked out.

Back at Vance's place, I searched the yellow pages in desperation for an answer to my spiritual dilemma. Just as I felt like throwing the phone book across the room, I noticed something I had never seen before—the words "Bahá'í Faith."

I dialed the number and a man told me about a "fireside" that evening on campus at 7:00 p.m.

Vance and I decided to go. So we did, but no one showed up. One would think we would leave, but we just sat there waiting. At around 10:00 p.m., a man came rushing around the corner with his arms full of books. "Are you Sheri?" I nodded and he led us into a small classroom. He apologized that he had forgotten it was a holiday and the meeting had been canceled. He was a shoe salesman at Nordstrom's and had just gotten off work. He didn't think it odd that we had waited three hours.

"I don't want to waste your time, so tell me what you are looking for," he said.

I started my laundry list of criteria for a spiritual path. When I finished he handed me a small card with a list of ten principles. Everything that I mentioned was on the list. I was shocked but excited.

"It's getting late, so why don't we do this." He pushed three books across the table. "Take these, and while reading them, ask yourself three questions: Is Bahá'u'lláh crazy? Is he evil? Or, is he who he says he is? You're smart, you can figure it out." He grinned, "How does that sound?"

I picked up the books, took a look, and then said, "Sounds perfect."

The man, named Ray, wrote his phone number on the little card of principles, and slid it over to me. "Give me a call when you are ready to talk."

I nodded.

That night I stayed up and read all three books. Every half-hour or so, I would call Vance on the phone and read him a quote. By morning we were both Bahá'ís.

I remembered how after our marriage, Bill had said once that I was not really a Bahá'í. He said the difference was that religious people "practice" religion instead of just thinking and talking about it. He was right. All those years I had rationalized that I was too sick to be a good Bahá'í, so I remained "inactive" in order to avoid the responsibility for my actions. It's funny that it was my atheist husband who had pulled the veil from my eyes. I realized that the Bahá'í community needed me as much as I needed them.

Everyone needs community, but those with a rhythm variation often find themselves isolated and lonely. I have struggled with isolation from the Bahá'í community for years. I am unable to attend consistently, and beat myself up thinking I am a "bad" Bahá'í. Due to feelings of humiliation, I avoided contact with the community almost completely, which then deepened my struggle. Finally, I went to the Local Spiritual Assembly* and explained to them about my illness and asked for guidance on how to feel a part of the community. At the time, I felt overwhelmed with recurring thoughts of suicide. They thanked me for coming, and offered a counselor to meet with me during this time of depression. They suggested that I bring a blanket and pillow to meetings, in case I felt ill and wanted to lie down. They also offered to arrange rides to for me so that I wouldn't have to drive to functions. They reassured me I need not feel guilty for missing meetings due to illness. I could keep in touch by phone, or Bahá'ís could visit me. I followed all of their suggestions and found I could handle this area of my life more smoothly. With the support and encouragement of the Assembly, I was able to let go of the notion of being a "bad" Bahá'í.

I was startled out of my reverie when the woman next to me on the plane offered me half of her sandwich. I accepted it, we talked a bit, and then I went back to my thoughts.

Bahá'ís often meet in the evenings, and after a full day I do not always feel well. I have an autoimmune disorder and my symptoms are flu-like—weakness, shakiness, and a sore throat—which cause me to need to lie down. Now I can take the chance of going to

---

* A Bahá'í administrative institution composed of nine elected members operating at the local level. It is elected according to Bahá'í principles and is responsible for coordinating and directing the affairs of the Bahá'í community in its area of jurisdiction.

meetings, because I know it is all right to lie down if needed. I learned that often isolation is self-created and communication with the community may resolve many of the obstacles I feel in connection to it.

After the plane landed, Bill caught up with me. He was all smiles because he had sat next to a physicist who was also an evangelical Christian. For an atheist, this was a hard one to wrap his head around. How could a physicist be a fundamentalist Christian? Bill said he was a great guy, but I assumed he still gave his lecture about how religions were myth. I'm glad I wasn't there.

Finally, I stood at the foot of the white stone stairs and looked up at the 190-foot, white-filigree-domed Bahá'í House of Worship. I looked behind to see Bill's reaction. He was already trotting off with his digital camera to the manicured gardens. I smiled and started climbing the stairs that encircled the base of that magnificent structure. So unique, every Bahá'í temple has nine doors to symbolize all the world religions. As I climbed the stairs, I remembered when I first became a Bahá'í and visited the temple forty years earlier. There were no gardens, just snow. Today, the sun gleamed and the nine gardens surrounding the temple seemed to glow.

I opened one of the large doors and walked inside with so much gratitude. What a wonderful gift to the world, for the House of Worship was not just for Bahá'ís, but for all people to come and worship, pray, meditate, or simply sit in an ethereal space.

As I sat down, I looked up at the lacy dome, the light streaming through and falling upon me, opening my heart.

Another memory caught my attention. In 1969, my senior year at Roseburg Senior High, there was a school assignment posing the question: "What do you want to do for your life work?" I had never thought about the future and what work I might do. I can still feel my excitement when drawing the domed building over and over, compulsively, before I had even heard the word Bahá'í. In each drawing there was the huge dome in the center of the city with the wonderful gardens, so green with shrubs and grass. Each of the gardens also had a reflecting pool. At the outside edge of the gardens were social, educational, and medical buildings.

For me, the assignment wasn't about a paid job, but more about something that would somehow impact my life. It surprised me that an imaginary building could start a yearning.

I looked over at the entrance and saw Bill wandering around the large interior and ending up next to me. He gave me a kiss on the cheek, and joined the silence. I smiled at him and took his hand, which he squeezed. There are two things that help me daily to cope—the Bahá'í Faith and Bill's love.

Developing some basic rules helped Bill and me. We agreed ahead of time that when we stated these rules we would immediately surrender to them, and feel love and compassion for each other, starting fresh at that moment to follow the rules.

Our rules are: to have Saturday talks every week to discuss the week before and the week to come, so no problem gets out of control; to value people more than things; to value sleep, which means not talking about problems late at night. These rules make us remember the depth of our love and the superficiality of our anger.

Journal Entry

In my youth I was embalmed in romance. I feel remorse over lost time and misdirected relationships; however, even mistakes can teach. Mine have taught me humility and given me a constant reminder to remain conscious. Remorse is my gargoyle, ugly to the senses, guarding my soul from vainglory, while I go out into the world meeting all the struggling people who turned out to be, to my surprise, myself, again and again.

A total culture-based lifestyle is a life without soul, without Self. Relationships are arbitrary, like ricocheted bullets, a danger for random injury. Relationships must be conscious and connect at the heart and soul. This way the relationship is not vulnerable to culture's random ways.

Relationships are connections to life. All types of relationships are needed for a full life. Relationships with spouse and family, Bahá'í assembly and community, employers and coworkers have kept me out of my head.

Chapter 34

For several years, everything Bill and I did together seemed so perfect—bike riding, hiking, dancing. But then my illness started to strip away my ability to participate. My fear took over and I believed he would leave me. But he didn't. I found he stayed because he loved *me,* not the activities.

Over seventeen years we built a sanctuary. Our relationship held something unique from other relationships. We belonged together in a way neither of us could define. This new way of being together felt indestructible even when our basic beliefs moved farther and farther apart. Him an atheist and me a devoted Bahá'í, we agreed to disagree and no longer judged each other. The word "mate" took on an organic feel, not sexual, not intellectual, but something deeper. It was certainly love. We were grateful for each other.

His awareness about himself gave me space to deal with my disorder. Things went smoothly for around ten years, until I had to quit work suddenly due to an autoimmune disorder, which did not get along with the bipolar disorder, and Bill suffered a brain aneurism.

I had gone down to visit my parents for a week. Then Bill drove down to Roseburg on Thanksgiving Day. The next morning we drove the three-hour trip home to Portland. When we got home, Bill started his daily workout, and I took my daily nap. I woke when I heard a loud thud. I yelled out to Bill, "Are you OK?" His answer was, "NO." I rushed into the hallway and found him lying very awkwardly on the floor, looking up at me with crossed eyes. I called

911 and they came to help ten minutes later. I rode in the ambulance with him, constantly crying, "Will he be all right?"

When we got to the hospital emergency room, we were put into a small cubical with a bed, and a curtain around it for privacy. The nurse was in and out, and gave Bill two shots of morphine. He asked me over and over, "Can you get me an aspirin, I have this terrible headache." I tried to tell him about the two shots of morphine, but he continued to ask for aspirin.

A few hours later, Bill was taken up to Neurosurgery. The surgeon came to me; did I want the old style surgery where they open up his brain to stop the bleeding, or a new platinum coil vascular technique, only three years old, which was less invasive? I chose the new technique.

Surgery started my month-long vigil in the ICU. I stayed with him until I broke down emotionally and physically. Then I would call a friend to take me home. This happened twice. The rest of the time I sat with him, only going home to feed the cats and shower. The Bahá'ís cooked for me and did my laundry. The doctor said Bill had a three percent chance of survival, so I read the Long Healing Prayer* over and over.

Bill was considered a bit of a mystery—the nurse had given him the same drugs as the other patients, and while they were unconscious, Bill was not.

He lost his short term memory. His headache was a ten on the pain scale and he was still smiling. Amazing! He was working from his reptilian brain and never lost his kindness, which raises the question: "Are lizards amiable?"

As he grew stronger I was allowed to wheel him along with the IV and the brain drain (a tube sticking out of the top of his head to

---

* An appellation often used to refer to a prayer revealed by Bahá'u'lláh, the Prophet and Founder of the Bahá'í Faith. The prayer, originally written in Arabic, contains supplications for healing and protection. See *Bahá'í Prayers,* Wilmette IL: Bahá'í Publishing Trust, 2002.

drain fluid off and keep the pressure down) to the sky bridge before going home. During the last trip to the sky bridge, Bill confided in me that his perceptions were still messed up. He said, "I don't know what is real, everything is confused in my head." I bent over the wheelchair to hold him and said, "What is real right now is us, the rest will come in time. We love each other, and this experience will make us stronger."

And it did.

I laughed and remembered the visit from Bill's surgeon. Dr. Jones asked Bill if he had any questions. Bill said, "What's my prognosis?" and the doctor explained he would make a full recovery. A few seconds later, Bill asked again, "What's my prognosis?" This so-called conversation, continued with Bill forgetting what had happened, and the doctor trying again. Then the doctor looked at me, and said, "Your wife can explain" and quickly left the room.

The next Thursday, they decided to send him home. The insurance ran out. The doctor gave a prescription for a wonder drug, without which Bill would not live. He needed it for the next five days to keep his brain from exploding. The cost was $500 for the week. I started to tremble, realizing that we had no money. I said I wouldn't leave with him until I had enough samples to give me a few days to find the money. So off the nurses went to find samples. I still was unsure if I could really take care of him. What if the exhaustion of the twenty-four-hour care led to a breakdown for me? Then who would care for him? But there was no other choice, so I took the samples and my husband home.

On the way up to the apartment, I stopped to check the mailbox. There wasn't much there, but a card from a woman I hadn't seen since I was ten. The card was surprising, but the $500 check was the mind-blower! She said she had met my mom in Fred Meyer's and Mom told her about our situation, though neither knew about the need of money for the medication.

"This is a gift, not a loan," she wrote.

Chapter 35

Jim, my older brother, and I decided to place Mom and Dad into assisted living. Mom's dementia and Parkinson's had progressed past the ability for them to take care of themselves. I thought Dad would object. However, after Jim told him about the place, he perked up and wanted to go see it right away. Dad loved it and said he looked forward to moving in. He had always demanded to stay in the house and care for Mom, but reality changed his mind.

The first step to placing them in Oak Park Assisted Living was to apply for Medicaid for Mom. My brother and I drove over to the senior center and talked to a woman about what we needed to do. She suggested that we all go in the conference room to talk. She excused herself and went to find the director because he had the keys. When they returned, I almost fainted.

"Charlie?" I softly questioned.

"Sheri?" A big grin spread over his face. I just stood there with my mouth open. *Ah-oh.*

After the Medicaid assistance, Mom was approved and I spent time talking with Charlie about the twelve years since I had last seen him. He married and divorced a few years back. I told him about my marriage to Bill. After talking about some loose ends related to our relationship, I realized we had little in common except compassion for each other.

Within a week, Mom and Dad were settled in their new home. Mom kept disappearing and was often found sleeping in someone's room on their couch, but things were better for Dad. A month later, Mom fell in the cafeteria due to a stroke and never walked again.

Her Parkinson's and dementia took all our courage. She believed that Dad had committed suicide. Every day she would confront him, "Why did you do it?" Dad tried to convince her he was still alive. Mom looked at Dad and said, "You can't fool me, I see what you are all doing." She felt abandoned by us and we could not console her, nor could we console ourselves.

Dad was losing weight (185 lbs to 116 lbs). He had late-stage lung disease and heart troubles, but no matter how bad he felt, he still visited Mom every day at her memory unit.

Mom's condition had grown worse and now when we visited she mostly didn't seem to care. She was in her own world. Mom had slipped from a confident woman, somewhat serious, always actively involved in projects to a now empty vessel. The woman I had loved was gone. Occasionally she would look at me and say "I haven't done enough." She had shrunk to the size of a small girl and I loved to hold her and kiss her on the top of her head. Her hair was salt and pepper, thin, and lay close to her skull. No more weekly visits to the hairdresser for a variety of red bouffants.

One night I received a call while at home in Gresham that she had fallen out of bed and broken her hip. We drove the next day to Roseburg to sit by her side. Because she no longer walked, the doctors had decided not to fix her hip and she remained in great pain. When the caregiver touched her, Mom would scream and I would have to rush from the room unable to bare the reality of her agonizing life.

Hospice was called in and they medicated her into a sleeping state, no longer eating or drinking. We got the call a short time later that she had passed. I can't recall who called, Dad or Jim. In fact, I don't remember the trip down to Roseburg or the arrangements for the memorial. I was in a daze and my medications made me unable to cry.

After the memorial, I do remember asking Dad if he wanted a spiritual memorial for himself, or if he would prefer something secular. He said, "I believe. Anyone with half a brain can tell that there is something really big going on!" I felt so close to him at that moment, but most of the time I felt very distant from everyone. There was a silence to the world. My mother was gone.

After her death, Dad started to slide toward his own. We live in the Portland, Oregon area and for the past seven years, we have continued to make the three-hour car trips to Roseburg in order to comfort him. We go once a month and it never seems enough time.

As life-test after life-test assaulted me from many directions, I learned that the key to holding on was to see these stressors as opportunities to work on virtues. This is a very big part of Bahá'í life. The purpose for this is not just to be a "goody two-shoes," but to build a strong foundation of character that can withstand whatever life throws at us. Some of these virtues are: courage, patience, compassion (for self and others), humor, and honesty. There are so many virtues that life can teach, if one is willing. They give my life meaning. I have learned that even with mental illness, the way I frame my life is vital.

One way that I continue to grow in virtues is by prayer and meditation every morning and evening—a private time for me to refocus my small troubled life toward a higher and more inspiring goal. It reminds me that I am part of a world movement to bring humanity to maturity and peace.

There is no cure for bipolar disorder, so I must take medication to help stabilize and minimize my episodes. Recently, Abilify has helped stabilize my moods, but unfortunately one side effect is obesity. I gained around sixty pounds in a very short period of time. I have struggled and since lost fifteen pounds, but Abilify doesn't seem to want me to lose any more. With the obesity, my triglycerides and cholesterol are now at unhealthy blood levels. It leaves me in the dilemma of choosing between depression and obesity, and the diseases that obesity can cause.

Another big stressor for me was going on SSDI (Social Security Disability Insurance) and not working. The last two part-time jobs I had, I lost due to short-term memory problems and my inability to multitask. I wanted to work as a means to building a better society, but my doctor said "no more."

I remember as a young girl, maybe thirteen, sitting alone, rocking in our living room, reading a Nancy Drew mystery. I can still feel the sun shining through the large pane window, warming my face. Nancy Drew was my role model. She always discovered the truth no matter what the danger. I can remember knowing I was pure and good and would never lie to feel safe. Then I grew up and was diagnosed with bipolar disorder.

As the years passed, my disorder kept getting worse. I remember, more than once, driving down Interstate 5, screaming from rage. One time, in my studio apartment, I even cursed the source of all creation for my life and utter aloneness. I desperately wanted a physical God to hold and comfort me. I don't remember all of the words I screamed, but if there were such a thing as a vengeful God, I am sure I would not have survived. After I ran out of energy screaming, I fell into a heavy sleep. As I woke, before my mind engaged in thought, I felt the universe wrap around me in the most organic way, from the smallest particles up through the totality of space, filled with stars. The amazing part was, I felt amusement and love permeating and holding the atoms in my body together. I cried and rocked that night, thankful to finally have my soul comforted. It was only at moments like that, I could truly rest.

But nothing lasts, comfort or pain. If I dig deep enough into pain I can come out into comfort. And when the comfort ceases, I just hang through another cycle of pain. So, though I am always aware of death and often fantasize about suicide, I hold on. I daily conjure the courage to face my life and my death like everyone else, not knowing anything for sure.

I build my life like a sandcastle—delicate and precious—with fear, knowing a wave might wash it away at any second. There is no predicting a wave, no controlling an ocean. I am in a strange dilemma, building in spite of the odds. I consciously live where life and death touch, sometimes softly, sometimes with fear.

> The second attribute of perfection is justice and impartiality. . . . It means to consider the welfare of the community as one's own. It means, in brief, to regard humanity as a single individual, and one's own self as a member of that corporal form, and to know of a certainty that if pain or injury afflicts any members of that body, it must inevitably result in suffering for all the rest.
> —'Abdu'l-Bahá, *The Secret of Divine Civilization,* ¶71

Here's where my integrity got lost: My counselors warned me against telling potential employers about my illness. I lived one lie of omission after another in order to get jobs. Because of the cyclical nature of mental illness, even with total effort and all my will, my work performance varied more than today's business managers generally allow. This workplace expectation quickly reduced me to a smart mental patient who couldn't hold down a job, not even a job I would have excelled at under healthier and more humane circumstances. This situation causes people to miss the fact that, due to my creativity and intelligence, I am often able to do more than imagined. Isn't that worth exploring?

Meaningful work is important for self-respect. I want to work. I just can't do it alone. I need cooperation, openness, flexibility, and respect—reasonable accommodation. But that is nearly impossible to find. When my secret is out, I'm out. There is no deeper pain than the world throwing you away. Just look into the eyes of those that society has turned away from, walking the streets.

I hope this time of great change in society will spread into the workplace and allow those of us with mental illness to do our part with real jobs, a living wage, and our value as people. Only this sort of revolutionary transformation in society will stop the constant stream of wasted talents and actions—wasted lives.

Chapter 36

My self-disappointments, my anger at the rigidity of the workplace, my empathy toward others with invisible disabilities, kindle my commitment to public and professional education about this "madness" in the workplace and how we as a society might turn it into an opportunity for creativity and mental health.

I joined the National Alliance on Mental Illness (NAMI) in May of 2012. I attended a training so I could participate in the "In Our Own Voice Program" (IOOV). This is a program where those with mental illness are encouraged to tell their story to a group of people looking for more understanding. It was a very fulfilling experience.

I also attended two more trainings: Peer-to-Peer mentoring and Peer Support Specialist training. I hope in the next year to have a paid position supporting those who are just released from Oregon State Hospital.

I had to give up Abilify due to the cost. First, I had a short manic episode while attending a four-day conference in Seattle. I struggled through the rest of the conference by skipping some of the lectures I had hoped to hear.

Right after the conference, I drove with Jim to Roseburg, for a visit with my Dad. I stayed a week. Dad was so thin he looked like a spider more than a human. So when I went home, I dropped into a state of depression that lasted all summer and fall.

Journal Entry

I am bored and disappointed. I sleep a lot. I have things to do: clean the kitchen, do ceramics or sew, but I can't find motivation or even a good attitude about doing anything. I go for long stretches in this form of depression where nothing in life interests me. There is a wish to disappear. This type of depression comes on suddenly and lifts just as quickly, but not knowing when it will lift is the torment.

Medication changes don't seem to work for me in this state. And don't say I am just lazy or I'll get angry—angry because I am so frustrated at these times. Such long stretches of dullness are almost worse than the acute depressions that bring out my "self-murderer," which tries to end it all. Suicidal thoughts are urges that I can grab onto and wrestle with, but the wish to disappear is like an ethereal itch that makes me crazy.

I am an artist, or at least I do art well enough that people buy it sometimes. I am smart, with a four-point master's degree in psychology and physical education. That's why doing nothing boils my blood. I get things done and when I don't, it feels like a trap of meaninglessness. Meaningful work is important to my quality of living. Without it, I feel like an empty clay vessel. When I'm in this state, I wonder why I can't care about the hugeness of the universe or the smallness of the quantum world, much less a TV show or an acclaimed novel.

I call my depressions the Nothingness because I am dumped into a void and forced to wait it out. My blessings, which I remember are many, float out of reach. Memories of how it felt to live a full life with love and joy taunt me from a distance. When my cat sits on my lap to cuddle, I push him away.

My husband is vigilant about fixing me during these periods. "Want to watch a movie or download a book to your Kindle?" My answer is only a slow head shake. I know this behavior change is hard on him and it does no good to tell him "you can't fix me, we have to wait." My husband and I agree family or friend(s) can't relate to what is happening inside me, a bipolar person who is disassociated from their daily experience. Normal people are always engaged in some way with what is going on around them. They feel and care, move and accomplish. How can their ill loved one not!

My advice to family and friends is patience, a virtue we all need to develop. It is important to watch for signs of deepening or more agitated depression. Be sure that ill loved ones are taking their medications, and support them by gently inviting them to join you in daily activities, but don't push. Check in and see if they are having thoughts of suicide and if so, call the doctor. But, beyond that, what can you do? If you can't relate to their state of mind, how can you take corrective measures?

And what can I do? It is not always true that if you smile you feel better. Yet I do make gentle efforts to straighten the kitchen or listen to music. I will admit that sometimes it does help just to make a start. Willpower is helpful only in short bursts, for prolonged illness—not so much. Inner strength, do I dare say that it can develop when in the Nothingness? Yes, by self-compassionate persistence from within.

As far as I know, after forty years of bipolar disorder, these bored and disappointed times can't be forced. Others will have all kinds of really good advice, but when they say "Let go and let God," I say "How do I let go of my void?"

Chapter 37

I was hospitalized with suicidal thoughts after attending a humorous speech contest.

The hospital had a bed and I was admitted in five hours. Bill kept taking walks to pass the time, but I was in an unreal place and just lay on the gurney without the presence of time passing.

I settled into my single room in the psych ward. I just sat there for a couple of hours. Finally, the psychiatrist came. He looked like a Hollywood actor with neatly combed black hair and a symmetrical face. He sat with his legs crossed and never smiled. "How long do you want to stay?"

"As long as it takes to get me stabilized on medications. I was on lithium twice in my early twenties, so I thought that might work."

"OK, I will start you on lithium and Wellbutron. How's that?"

After he left, a social worker came in to talk. She seemed mostly concerned that I was a Bahá'í. "But what about Christ?"

"Bahá'ís believe in Christ."

"Oh, OK," she said, calming down.

After she left, I rocked on my bed while thinking how I wanted to die. There was a knock on the door and a woman rushed into the room with a look of concern on her face. "I saw you on the video rocking and thought I should check on you."

"What video? You guys watch me when I undress?"

"It's for your safety. You seem sad, can I pray for you?"

"Ah, I guess. Yes."

She fell to her knees and grasped my arms and a very long evangelical prayer poured out. I felt like pulling away, but I didn't. Then she left.

I was started on my new meds, and two days later released. When I got home I became ill from the meds and it only got worse as time went on, so I stopped them.

I called my brother and asked if he could help me pay for Abilify. He said, "I'd love to."

I visited my med nurse and she put me back on Abilify and switched the antidepressant to Zoloft. I felt normal in a week. My med nurse warned me that to mix Zoloft and Prozac, while changing medications, could cause mania. She urged me, "Please call if you see any signs of mania."

I laughed and said, "I'll call, but not until I get my apartment cleaned."

My father's health took a turn for the worse, so I went to Roseburg. I was on I-5 when I received a call from my brother, telling me that Dad had just passed. It was Christmas Day. Christmas was Mom's favorite holiday and it made me feel better knowing that it was the day of their reunion.

After a few months on Abilify, I no longer felt as though my life was a waste and a burden. Western society loses an amazing amount of human resources by not accepting the varied rhythms of disabled individuals. However, the Bahá'í community is a new and more flexible culture rising out of the hearts of humanity at this time. I consider myself blessed to have found the Bahá'í Faith, my sanctuary.

Journal Entry

Soul Space is the Gap between Self and Culture.

My soul space is my responsibility. I must keep it clutter-free as best I can. Virtues are our filters. They give a space to feel fully, to comprehend and to decide upon right-action. Soul space is the only safe place in life and you can't take it for granted, or culture will bury you.

Culture can be wonderful but it must be sifted, guided, and reflected upon to be useful to the soul. I want to live my life, not a knee-jerk reaction to culture.

Ironically, the first step to becoming aligned with society in a healthy way is to build in some distance. I learned the hard way that I must have a soul space between my innermost being and the culture. No one can become an integrated human being (individuation), connected to society, unless they have choices, and if you are completely submerged in culture the culture automatically choreographs all your responses. And let's face it, Western culture is out of control in many ways. Without your soul space, where you have a place to consciously decide before acting versus just reacting, life can quickly grow muddled.

So how does one go about building a soul space? To do this, there must be a filtering system to filter out cultural debris, keeping you clear and open to creativity at its deepest level.

It is my belief that spiritual virtues are the stronghold that can keep your soul space clear of cultural dysfunction. These virtues act as a filtering system and become a powerful foundation to a healthy life-rhythm.

Which virtues? There are many: love, compassion, patience, discernment, courage, faithfulness, truthfulness, etc., that act as a template. When used properly, they allow only cleansed cultural information to enter the soul space for action.

How does this work? We have a culture that is distorted by all kinds of prejudice and bias, which must be filtered out through love, unity, and compassion. Then a clarity prevails internally, no matter what life hands you.

We are social beings whose life purpose includes developing an ever-advancing civilization. Culture is a living process that evolves, and waste products must be continually filtered, otherwise an ecological spiritual disaster awaits.

Due to either the rejection of old religions or fanatical adherence, the learning of these virtues has stumbled. That is why the way to a healthy life is to take these virtues, not as a judgmental base, but as a guide to cleansing out the debris we are entangled with in the twenty-first century.

Virtues are not adopted behaviors, but spiritual attributes that lay dormant to seek, identify, develop, and lovingly share with society.

Daily practice of these virtues will give you the soul space needed to walk a healthy path even if we find ourselves in a dance between society's rigid biases and our invisible disabled needs. This does not guarantee success at our goals but it does give us a sound foundation to work from.

Soul space is a luxurious place of solitude, it is a bubble to safely ride out life's waves.

My soul space practice consisted of meditation and reflection on the Bahá'í writings, visualization about positive outcomes to potential situations, and making conscious choices as obstacles arise.

How did I discover that I had no soul space and that this was wounding me?

I always felt washed away by what people thought of me. I would come into a new situation and almost instantly find myself reacting in a pattern that had long proven hurtful to myself and others, yet unable to resist. I was always carried away from my center of self, which was not clearly defined.

For example, I would meet a man and feel an overpowering attraction. I was immediately attached and molding my life to his needs and there was no space for me to stop and take a close look at his character or the healthiness of the relationship. I was swept away and left holding my breath just hoping (not directing) all would turn out well, which it had no chance of doing. Good relationships are not a result of luck, they take a strong soul space in both partners.

For me, after many years of struggle and hurt, I woke up with a soul space that gave me the clarity to choose my own direction. How it got there was more an unconscious process of trial and error, very painful, which took about two decades. After taking more consciously active control of my soul space, I realized this approach from a younger age would have allowed me to avoid a lot of the pain I'd gathered due to lack of clarity. But no matter the age, from the time the soul space is defined your life improves.

I don't mean to romanticize manic depression but it has changed me for the better. Mental illness is tragic and miserable. However, lying in deep depression, I experienced a sort of ego death which, when recovered from, enabled my heart to go out more readily to even a lone person on the street. Compassion multiplied. And after mania, where all my senses were on fire, a cool breeze on my arm brought me great joy. Gratitude multiplied.

"Your challenge now is to sort through it, to separate the wheat from the chaff, to isolate where you were onto something good and important, and then to figure out how to use those clues to reorient your life. The challenge is to find the deep meaning in your madness, to let that meaning flow through your whole life, to grow from your madness in ways that you couldn't possibly have grown without it. If you manage to do that, you will find that your illness wasn't a meaningless detour but in fact the most important, most fulfilling event in your life."
—Russell Shorto, *Saints and Madmen,* p. 16

Appendix A

Employer Perspective on Working with Sheri

This Much I think Is True—Reflections from Charla Hayden, Manager of Training and Development at OHSU, who supervised Sheri Medford, Graphics Designer and Training Support Specialist, from January 1997 through September 1999.

The woman in front of us looked about thirty-two. She was stylishly dressed in a brown suit with a short skirt, textured hose, and trendy shoes. Her presentation of herself was girlish. Her voice was light and she seemed a bit nervous in the situation though her responses to the job interview questions were on target and spoke clearly to her skills and knowledge. I was struck by what I experienced as a contrast between the way she represented herself stylistically and the content of what she said. I was put off a bit by this contrast and began to be skeptical about wanting to select her for the job—something didn't jibe.

After a few more questions, she casually mentioned being forty-seven years old and wanting to do something more interesting with her work life. This certainly got my attention since my perception of her age had been much different. In fact, I couldn't believe what I had heard but it seemed inappropriate to pursue this point further.

After the interview, my then boss and I sat down to decide which of the interviewees to offer the position to. He was clearly in favor of selecting the applicant described above. Since I was new in my own role I was reluctant to speak about my misgivings related to what I felt were inconsistencies between her manner and her age and experience. So I agreed to his idea that he would offer her the vacant support position we had. This was the way Sheri Medford became a colleague of mine and an important part of my development as a manager, although at that point there was little that suggested that would be true.

All the Good Stuff (of which there was much)

The good points outweighed the difficulties when it came to working with Sheri Medford for two and a half years. Let me tell you all the good things.

Sometimes it was sheer joy to work with someone with so much developed insight about herself and others. Much of the time she engaged the rest of us in such an unguarded way that it was impossible not to be the same with her. She is so bright, so candid, so disclosing. Sometimes I wanted to tell her to be more careful, to remind her that the world at large doesn't tolerate expressed vulnerability that well, that there are souls among us who see such vulnerability as an opportunity to attack, to take out one more competitor for the scarce, nurturing resources of the planet.

Sheri's competence at the work was awesome. Often I felt that if she could throw off the burden of her illness she would outpace any of the rest of us at teaching, at thinking, at producing learning materials. She was always interested in the "why" behind assignments, always wanted to talk about the ideas, said she learned from reading what the rest of us wrote and taught. She frequently asked to attend the training classes we presented because she was interested in developing her knowledge and skills.

Creativity and humor often characterized her work. Given carte blanche to design the layout and graphics for a set of learning materials, Sheri usually developed amusing, engaging, off-beat, and relevant characters to illustrate our productions. Her design work gave me pleasure personally, and I was always proud to tell class participants that the originator of our materials was right in our own office. Her work was always professional, though never stuffy.

Possibly the quality Sheri brought to her work that pulled her through thick and thin over the time she was here was her sense of responsibility. She always, always knew what a good job was in terms of her own work and always worked conscientiously to meet those standards. I never knew her to make an excuse, to use her illness as a buffer against her own, and my, expectations. Occasionally I had to caution her against berating herself for an error or an unaccomplished task. I have never seen her work ethic surpassed or her willingness to own her culpabilities for a work problem.

Sheri's determination to utilize her abilities at increasing levels of challenge was always clear and easy to support. After she had revealed her illness to me, she talked about the internal frustration of not being able to do what she knew she had in her. I watched and encouraged her while she took a many-months-long desktop publishing course through a University of Oregon outreach program. Going to her graduation and seeing the work she had produced, and knowing it ranked with one or two others at the top of her class, confirmed her comprehension of how good she was capable of being at her profession.

She kept us organized. One of Sheri's most interesting work behaviors was that periodically she would go through the office like a dervish. Anything not attached to a wall or a table was in danger of being reclassified as waste. Sheri had a passion for order, which led to her work area being the neatest in the department. Sheri organized and reorganized herself and the rest of us, dozens of times. Mostly it was to our collective benefit. Sheri foresaw organizing mechanisms we would need when new projects came along before anyone else, and provided structure for those. Occasionally I worried that the compulsion for neatness and order was dangerous to her, and to some of our department's material holdings, but that never proved to be true.

All the Difficulties (of which there were plenty)

It was very hard not knowing that Sheri had a serious mental illness when she first began to show signs of it. Though I later came to understand clearly why she had chosen not to tell us when she was hired, the first time there was an episode she couldn't fully manage, it was very troubling. Keats (the former manager of Training and Development) and I didn't know what to do. And this happened very soon, essentially in reaction to the transition required when she started this new role. For a while Sheri was working half-time in her old job in research and half-time in her job with us. For anyone, I think, it's unnerving to hold two half-time jobs. For Sheri, it seemed especially trying. She also developed a bad cold during this transition time, which made things worse. It was a fairly long time before I came to understand that physical vulnerability was something she didn't tolerate well. It interacted with her long-term illness in a way that really frightened her. From what I observed, if the viability of her life appeared uncertain to her, her emotional distress increased hugely.

I had to develop a way of seeing the patterns and cycles of her illness. It sometimes felt that my challenge here was to see a difficult time in its infancy so I could give her feedback and also plan for the work processes to go ahead without her full engagement. I did feel proud once or twice that she didn't have to go into the hospital— that together (meaning Sheri, her psychiatrist, and I) had seen it coming soon enough to implement other remedies. Learning to see transitions in store for Sheri, either at work or personally, learning to see the beginning of physical illnesses, and other trigger points for her emotional distress, became useful. I don't mean to imply that Sheri ever behaved irresponsibly or became dependent on me to monitor her illness. I think my learning to see the patterns was important to protect the work of the department and to prevent Sheri's descent into a worse emotional state.

Sometimes I had to live and work with the feeling that things were either out of control or about to go out of control in the department. At the beginning, or during a time when Sheri was in greater distress, I felt my role was to be patient, to hold steady, to contain my own anxiety and deal with the real, rather than the imaginary, concerns I had. This led me to think about the boundary between my obligation to assure that the tasks of the department were being accomplished with high quality and my obligation to accommodate Sheri's illness. Many times it was an intricate dance.

Sheri and I had to work out, over time, a way of communicating about what was happening. Sheri needed to find ways to indicate to me what was happening with her so that we could discuss how to handle the work while she worked with her illness. I had to be clear that it was never acceptable to me for our department to produce less than the best quality work we could. It never was acceptable to me for us to pretend there weren't problems. I think this led Sheri to a position that was more open and we began dealing with conditions more straightforwardly rather than on a superficial level that masked what was actually happening.

I had to define time and role boundaries more flexibly in relation to Sheri. Sometimes she would do her work manically, other times sluggishly. I had to focus on the outcome, not the manner of performance, and I had to see time as more elastic, not in the sense of not expecting her to be at work on time, but in terms of negotiating when things were to get done. In particular, I had to manage my time to be available to listen, and to consult her when she felt urgently that there was a problem.

There were several intervals when Sheri's state of mind was disrupted by her decision to go off her medications or to self-prescribe by trying different amounts and combinations of her medications. These times were always frustrating for me, although over time I began to understand why she did this. When she could tell me this was what was going on, it was always easier to understand. Typically she would make an appointment with her psychiatrist when she got into difficulty this way.

Reflections and Recommendations

For almost five years, I had worked for a boss who had manic-depressive illness. Though I didn't know her diagnosis for some time, I became familiar with her patterns of mania and depression, and learned how to interact with her in ways that got the work done and signaled to her that she'd better attend to herself before things at work deteriorated unalterably.

My experience in a supervisory role with Sheri was even more profound. I learned more and more deeply than I did in my previous experience. I think I finally, truly understand what it's like to have a serious, chronic mental illness. My own maternal grandfather, who committed suicide when my mother was thirteen, is thought to have been bipolar, and so I knew all the family lore. But it was this experience with Sheri that really grew my understanding. Here are some central tenets I found important to working things out at work with Sheri.

It is right and reasonable to expect, and to give, loyalty and commitment to a colleague with a mental illness.

It is right and reasonable to continue to expect high quality work—her/his personal best—from someone with a mental illness.

It is important to let yourself fully grasp the fear of humiliation and discrimination that exists in people in our culture who suffer from mental illness.

It is important to understand how onerous it feels to be on a continuous stream of medications to support your viable existence in life, and the drive to be free of them which leads to multiple experiments with going off of them.

It is important to find the person behind the mask of pretense that usually obscures the identity of a colleague with a chronic mental illness. Otherwise you are interacting with a chimera and nothing can be worked out.

It feels good to contribute to another person's increased stability, to support her/his dreams, to help further her/his education and job development.

And it is important to let the person go when she/he has learned from the job and from you what she/he can, and must move on in the interest of a more full professional life.

I miss Sheri Medford very much, but I take great pleasure in thinking of her out there somewhere pursuing her dreams and capturing more of her innate capacity in her work.

Appendix B

The Bahá'í Faith

The Bahá'í Faith is an independent world religion that began in 1844 in Persia (present-day Iran). Since its inception, the Faith has spread to 235 nations and territories and has been accepted by more than five million people. Bahá'ís believe that there is only one God, that all the major world religions come from God, and that all the members of the human race are essentially members of one family. Bahá'ís strive to eliminate all forms of prejudice and believe that people of all races, nations, social status, and religious backgrounds are equal in the sight of God. The Bahá'í Faith also teaches that each individual is responsible for the independent investigation of truth, that science and religion are in harmony, and that men and women are equal in the sight of God.

Resources and Contact Information:
www.bahai.us
www.bahai.org
www.bahaibookstore.com

Appendix C

Diagnostic Guidelines

"Let's look at the DSM IV, which is a physician's diagnostic guide."
He opened the book, placed it on the table and pointed. "These
are the guidelines for bipolar disorder. You probably recognize the
symptoms of depression, but let's go over them anyway."

Patient showing at least five of the following symptoms:

Depressed mood.

Markedly diminished interest or pleasure.

Significant weight loss or gain.

Insomnia or hypersomnia (sleeping too much).

Psychomotor agitation or retardation (observed by others, not
merely subjective feeling of restlessness or feeling slowed down).

Fatigue or loss of energy.

Diminished ability to think or concentrate or indecisiveness.

Feelings of worthlessness or excessive inappropriate guilt.

Recurrent thoughts of death, recurrent suicidal ideation, or
suicidal attempts.

A manic episode consists of a distinct period of abnormally elevat-
ed, expansive, or irritable mood.

Patient showing at least three of the following symptoms:

Inflated self-esteem or grandiosity.

Decreased need for sleep, e.g., feels rested after only three
hours sleep.

Distractibility.

Increase in goal-directed activity (either socially, at work or
school, or sexuality) or psychomotor agitation.

Excessive involvement in pleasurable activities that have a high potential for painful consequences—e.g. unrestrained buying sprees, sexual indiscretions, or foolish business investments, etc.

Other Books Available from Bahá'í Publishing

THE SCRIBE'S PROMISE
Jennifer Pollard
$18.00 US / $20.00 CAN
Trade Paper
ISBN 978-1-61851-070-9

A powerful story of forbidden love set in the spiritually charged atmosphere of nineteenth-century Persia.

The Scribe's Promise is the tale of Kapriel, a shy Armenian Christian scribe living in mid-nineteenth century Persia, who loves Mina, the sister of his Muslim neighbor, Rahma. And, although Rahma tolerates and shows some respect for Kapriel, the fact that Kapriel is not Muslim prevents him from being a suitable husband for Mina. Neither Rahma nor his family will allow their union, and Kapriel and Mina are unable to disobey her family or go against their culture's strict religious laws without facing dire consequences.

At this time, however, the winds of change are blowing in Persia, especially with the news that a merchant of Shíráz, Who calls Himself "the Báb," has begun teaching that He has brought a new revelation from God, which supersedes that of Muhammad's. Under the Báb's new teachings, the antiquated ways of Persia will be abolished and new ones laid down instead. Intrigued by this new promise, both Kapriel and Rahma decide to travel to find the Báb and perhaps speak to Him. Their journey will create a bond of friendship between them that they never thought could have existed, and their lives will be changed forever.

KYLE JEFFRIES, PILGRIM
Gail Radley
Illustrated by Taurus Burns
$11.00 US / $13.00 CAN
Trade Paper
ISBN 978-0-87743-712-3

A touching story for middle-grade readers about a young boy embarking on a Bahá'í pilgrimage with his family. Along the way, he learns much about his Faith and thinks deeply about his future.

Kyle Jeffries, Pilgrim is the tale of a little league baseball player who feels torn when he learns that his family's long-awaited pilgrimage to the Bahá'í World Center in Haifa, Israel, is coming up—it will mean his missing the All-Stars game. Although being in Israel is exciting, Kyle can't seem to stop thinking about everything that he's missing at home. To make matters worse, a lively smaller boy, Carlos, latches unto him almost as soon as the pilgrimage begins. The last thing Kyle wants to be is a babysitter!

But slowly the magic of the pilgrimage takes root in his heart. As Kyle and his family visit the Bahá'í holy sites around Haifa and 'Akká, Kyle learns what it really means to be a Bahá'í and how he can serve others by doing what he loves most.

DISCOVERING THE MOON
Jacqueline Mehrabi
Illustrated by Susan Reed
$12.00 US / $14.00 CAN
Trade Paper
ISBN 978-1-61851-072-3

Follow the story of a soon-to-be fifteen-year-old girl as she explores, through deep spiritual conversations with her loving family members, what it means to be in charge of her own spiritual destiny.

Discovering the Moon tells the story of a soon-to-be fifteen-year-old girl named Fern who lives on the remote Orkney Islands in northern Scotland. Fern's conversations with the members of her family soon open up a world of discovery regarding the importance of prayer. These conversations focus on discussing the Long Obligatory Prayer, one of three prayers that every Bahá'í over the age of fifteen is required to choose from and recite daily.

Author Jacqueline Mehrabi draws on her own experiences living in Scotland to create a lush, true-to-life setting for *Discovering the Moon*. In the Bahá'í Faith, the age of fifteen marks the end of childhood and the beginning of an individual's sole responsibility for the progress of his or her spiritual existence. Fern, by involving her family and friends in her exploration of deep spiritual themes, offers a great example of drawing on many generations and perspectives when working on self-discovery. *Discovering the Moon* asks deep questions and challenges readers, in a relatable and gentle way, to learn about the teachings and expectations of their own religious beliefs the same way that Fern does upon turning fifteen.

GLEANINGS FROM THE WRITINGS OF BAHÁ'U'LLÁH
Bahá'u'lláh
$24.00 US / $26.00 CAN
Hardcover
ISBN 978-1-61851-073-0

Selections from the chief writings of Bahá'u'lláh, the founder of the Bahá'í Faith.

Gleanings from the Writings of Bahá'u'lláh is an extremely important compilation that sets out the teachings of the Bahá'í Faith on a myriad of subjects. Among the themes that fall within its compass are the greatness of the day in which we live, the spiritual requisites of peace and world order, the nature of God and His Prophets, the fulfillment of prophecy, the soul and its immortality, the renewal of civilization, the oneness of the Manifestations of God as agents of one civilizing process, the oneness of humanity, and the purpose of life, to name only a few.

To those who wish to acquire a deeper knowledge and understanding of the Bahá'í Faith, *Gleanings* is a priceless treasury. To the members of the Bahá'í Faith, it has been a familiar companion for many decades, bringing spiritual fulfillment to countless people throughout the world. This new and exquisite hardcover edition includes paragraph numbering for easy reference, as well as a revised and expanded glossary.